The Legends Go On ...

THOMAS A. DORSEY, who died in 1993, was born in 1899, the frail, sickly son of an African-American preacher. He was healed by faith and lived to become a pianist, composer, and legend in both blues and gospel music.

LARNELLE HARRIS's beautiful voice thrilled 6,000 newly-liberated Russians in the Kremlin, just one week after the collapse of communism in their officially Godless country.

TWILA PARIS has been called the present-day Fanny Crosby. She began writing songs at age twelve and this inspired singer-songwriter is the fourth generation of gospel-spreaders in her family.

BILL AND GLORIA GAITHER teamed both professionally and matrimonially to become spectacularly successful singers, songwriters, and producers of religious musical videocassettes.

Gospel LEGENDS

CHET HAGAN

AVON BOOKS ◆ NEW YORK

"Someday, Somewhere" and "Peace in the Valley" are © Unichapel Music, Inc. "How Great Thou Art" by Rev. Carl Boberg, Sweden, Circa 1885–1886, translated into English by Stuart K. Rine, Circa. 1927. "The Wonder of It All" by George Beverly Shea, 1955 © Billy Graham Evangelistic Association. "He Touched Me" by Bill Gaither, © 1969 by Gaither Music. "Le Voyage" by Bob Farrell and Greg Nelson © Greg Nelson Music. "I Can Begin Again" by Larnell Harris/Dave Clark © Lifesong Music Press, BMI, First Roll Music, the John T. Benson Publishing Co. "I Choose Joy" by Larnell Harris © Lifesong Music, etc. "Go There With You" by Steven Curtis Chapman © 1992 by Careers/VMG Music Publishing, Nashville, TN. "Leave Me, Father, with the Staff of Life" by Johnny Cash, published by the House of Cash.

GOSPEL LEGENDS is an original publication of Avon Books. This work has never before appeared in book form.

AVON BOOKS
A division of
The Hearst Corporation
1350 Avenue of the Americas
New York, New York 10019

Copyright © 1995 by Chet Hagan
Cover photo by Redfern c/o Retina Ltd., New York
Published by arrangement with the author
Library of Congress Catalog Card Number: 94-96286
ISBN: 0-380-77695-2

First Avon Books Printing: April 1995

AVON TRADEMARK REG. U.S. PAT. OFF. AND IN OTHER COUNTRIES, MARCA REGISTRADA, HECHO EN U.S.A.

Printed in the U.S.A.

RA   10 9 8 7 6 5 4 3 2 1

To Lloyd Arthur Eshbach:
author, publisher, bibliophile, pastor,
steadfast friend, and all-around
Christian gentleman

Sing aloud to God our strength;
Make a joyful shout to the God of Jacob.
Raise a song and strike the timbrel,
The pleasant harp with the lute.
Play the trumpet . . .

—PSALM 81

Praise the Lord with the harp;
Make melody to Him with an instrument
of ten strings.
Sing to Him a new song;
Play skillfully with a shout of joy.

—PSALM 33

Contents

Preface

THERE IS NO SINGLE MORE DOMINANT THEME IN THE HIS-
tory of America than its Christian faith—a theme, ironically, often denigrated or ignored by historians. But
from that harsh December day of 1620 when the Pilgrims landed from the *Mayflower* to establish Plymouth
Plantation, to the present, when Americans are no
longer awed by contemporaries walking in the vast ex-
panse of space, that faith has persisted.

Sorely tested more times than can be counted, divided
into as many hues as a rainbow (and more), the faith has
survived witchcraft, revolution, slavery, civil war, westward expansion, foreign wars, court challenges and edicts,
political administrations of every competence and incom-
petence, sectism, fraudulent preachers, and the so-called
''ages'' of the last half of this troubled century: atomic,
space, computer, information.

Through it all—from the days before there was a
nation until now—the joys of faith have been expressed in songs having inextricable roots in the Old
Testament. In the Psalms, most of them were attributed to David, king of Judah and Israel, founder of
the Judaic dynasty of Jerusalem, popular hero, warrior, statesman, devout worshipper, musician, poet.
And, yes, sinner.

The Hebrew word for psalms is *tehillim,* or ''praise
songs,'' which they certainly were in David's time and
remain so today. There's an ancient rabbinical tale that

tells of King David's harp being hung above his bed at night so that night winds might sing through the strings as David composed the poetry that was kin to the natural (God-inspired?) music.

The importance of the Biblical Psalms to the development of Christian music during the Italian Renaissance and the Reformation cannot be overstated. Musicologists tell us that David's praise songs were "rediscovered" in new translations by French poet Clement Marot and given wide distribution in Italian and French royal courts as well as among English Protestants. In every sense the Psalms became the light of the Renaissance and Reformation.

Thus, on the day the Pilgrim Fathers—a mere thirty-seven of them—sailed on the *Mayflower* from Leyden, Holland, one of them wrote, "We refreshed ourselves, after tears, with singing of the psalms, making joyful melody in our hearts as well as with the voice, there being many of our congregation very expert in music; and indeed it was the sweetest melody that ever my ears heard."

That gives a very different picture of the Pilgrims than the somber, intolerant, almost joyless verbal portraits painted in the classroom history books of my youth. But the truth is that the original Pilgrims of the *Mayflower* were vastly different people—in education, mindset and culture—than other Puritans who followed them to the New World.

By way of simple explanation, the Pilgrims of Plymouth were Reformation exiles who wanted only to be by themselves to worship and live in their own way. And that included the joy found in singing the Psalms. On the other hand, the Puritans of the Bay Colony, also part of the Reformation exodus from England, formed a governing body intent on converting others to their way of worship or, failing that, imposing their way on others, often cruelly. Unhappily, it was that latter image that prevailed in much of the elementary school teaching of Pilgrim history a generation or two ago.

The Bay Colony Puritans did produce, starting in 1640, what was known as *The Bay Psalm Book,* the first full-length book published in North America. There was no music *per se* in the first edition; it simply printed the text of the Psalms. A ninth edition printed in 1698 boasted actual music. But musicologist Beatrice Hudson Flexner, herself a professional singer and instrumentalist, characterizes it as an "ugly little book, showing in every page the sad fall of Puritan song! Psalm translation made in rugged defiance of all poetic or musical cadence, and a miserable thirteen tunes, clumsily printed, with the names of the notes indicated by initials below the staffs, for the use of the illiterate."

Growing out of *The Bay Psalm Book* was the practice of what became known as "lining out," with the pastor reading the Psalms aloud, line by line, and the congregation repeating each line. Sadly, such stolid repetition removed the "music" from David's biblical poetry.

Nevertheless, "lining out" was to play a much larger role in American Christian music and worship as the continuing European invasion of immigrants pushed the colonies out into hills and valleys and forests and fertile farmland of the South and Midwest—far beyond the influence of the Massachusetts Puritans. The reality was that "lining out" became a necessary tool in church services because many of the worshippers could not read. But an even greater reality was that wherever the burgeoning nation went, its religious music went also.

Song was part of the revivalist "Great Awakening of 1740," during which its imported British leader, the

Reverend George Whitefield, would say, "I love those who thunder out the Word." It was part of the "Great Revival in the West," begun in Kentucky by evangelist James McGready in 1800, when "hymns were . . . yelled and stomped as much as sung."

It was spread far and wide by a dedicated coterie of singing teachers, who rode muleback to remote villages, churches, and schoolhouses. And when it became evident that the people who could *not* read music far outnumbered those who could, there were those among the teachers who produced the innovative "shaped note" technique. They replaced the traditional round notes of written music with specifically *shaped* notes to indicate each of the necessary syllables—do, re, me, fa, sol, la, si—of the familiar diatonic scale, which repeats the "do."

There were several methods used in the "shaped note" teaching but this is how the seven-syllable scale was "pictured" in one variation.

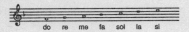

Broad dissemination of Christian music was part of Dwight L. Moody's "machine age" revival meetings in the last quarter of the nineteenth century, when song leader Ira Sankey's unique folios, *Sacred Songs and Solos* and *Gospel Hymns,* were sold in the millions to the faithful. In the first quarter of the twentieth century, music was a key ingredient of the flamboyant evangelism of one-time major league baseball player Billy Sunday, when singer-musician Homer Rodeheaver led hundreds of thousands in happy song as they trod the "sawdust trail" to salvation.

It was the underscoring, and moral underpinning, of the civil rights movement in the 1960s. It has been a major part of the worldwide televised crusades of evangelist Billy Graham, with the gospel songs presented to millions by the marvelous bass voice of George Beverly Shea.

And the *now* of gospel music finds it being presented in high-tech stereo, on laser-scanned compact discs, on tape cassettes (both audio and video), on electronic synthesizers—in every conceivable style: sacred, traditional, "pop," blues, jazz, soul, country, rock 'n roll, and even rap. And today there is a huge trade organization, the Gospel Music Association (headquartered in Nashville), which promotes the genre worldwide, maintains an annual televised awards program, and which has a Gospel Music Hall of Fame.

This is not an encyclopedic study of American gospel music; such an effort would require weighty multiple volumes. What is undertaken in these pages is a look at the heart and soul of this music through the dramatic stories of some of the most dominant personalities in gospel music—*legends* really, past and present—who performed in rural brush arbors, under colorfully striped circus tents, at summer camp meetings, in remote clapboard churches, at all-night sings "with dinner on the grounds," in the great halls of teeming cities, in huge stadia, on recordings, on radio, and on the far-reaching medium of television. What the subjects of this book have in common is that they, in their own unique ways, followed the biblical admonition to "sing to Him a new song."

The inspiring stories here, covering more than a few generations, deserve retelling in a single volume because, together, they form a tuneful mosaic of Christian America.

And one indisputable fact stands out: There is no older, no more resilient, no more demonstrative music in America than *gospel music!*

—Chet Hagan
Spruce Hill, Galen Hall
Pennsylvania
April 1995

1

Fanny J. Crosby

FRANCES JANE CROSBY WAS SIX WEEKS OLD AT THE END of April 1820. She was of a proud family; her ancestry traced back to one Simon Crosby, who had come to Boston from England in 1635. The future of the little baby seemed secure.

The end of the second decade of the nineteenth century was a good time to be born in America. James Monroe, who would be the last U.S. president to dress in eighteenth-century fashion, with silk stockings and silver buckles on his shoes and a braided queue hanging down the back of his head, was just starting his second term. Newspapers were calling it the "Era of Good Feelings." And why not? There was a vigorous nationalism in the air. Indiana, Mississippi, Illinois, and Alabama were new states, and the United States government had just bought the territory of Florida from Spain for a bargain price of five million dollars. The recently invented steam-powered loom was opening up new jobs in New England factories; eager, hardworking Irish immigrants were up to their knees in muck digging the Erie Canal, which would open the way to a great western expansion; and those newfangled steamboats were plying the major rivers of the nation, carrying adventurous passengers and tons of profit-making produce. It *was* a fine time to be alive.

Little Frances Jane, born in the town of Southeast, Putnam County, in upstate New York, had developed an eye infection and her worried mother, Mercy, took her to a doctor; the family doctor was away and a second physician was called upon. Hot poultices were prescribed and administered. But a terrible error was made. The poultices were *too* hot and the screaming baby was blinded! And it seemed that tragedy would continue to be visited upon the family. Before Frances Jane was a year old her father, John, died.

However, the adversities of her earliest days never seemed to dim Frances Jane's enthusiasm for life. Fanny (for that's what everyone called her) rode horses, climbed trees, and was generally the leader in neighborhood mischief. She also had a natural penchant for learning. Her mother began schooling at home by reading to her blind daughter; the Bible was the principal book used. Young Fanny soon began memorizing long passages from the Scriptures.

Years later the impact of that early religious training would become apparent. For one thing, she would write (at age eighty-three): "I have heard that this physician (whose error blinded me) never ceased expressing his regret at the occurrence. But if I could meet him now I would say, 'Thank you, thank you, for making me blind, if it was through your agency that it came about!' I mean it—every word of it; and if perfect earthly sight were offered to me tomorrow, I would not accept it. . . . Although it may have been a blunder on the physician's part, it was no mistake of God's. I believe it was His intention that I should live my days in physical darkness, so as to be better prepared to sing His praises and incite others to do so. I could not have written thousands of hymns if I had been hindered by the distractions of sight.''

That attitude about her blindness was not something arrived at in her old age. When she was only eight or nine, she wrote this:

> Oh, what a happy soul I am
>   Although I cannot see,
> I am resolved that in this world
>   Contented I will be.
>
> How many blessings I enjoy
>   That other people don't!
> To weep and sigh because I'm blind
>   I cannot nor I won't.

Certainly, she wasn't ''hindered'' by the blindness in her prodigious output of hymns or, more properly, gospel song lyrics. The exact number may never be known, because she wrote many of the poems under *noms de plume;* the pseudonyms, both male and female, exceeded two hundred. She herself believed she had written more than eight thousand song lyrics; other sources say it was more than nine thousand, perhaps as many as ten thousand.

Even today, her hymns are widely used in church hymnals; it is not unusual to find as many as fifty Crosby lyrics in a single hymnal. And there was a time that the Methodist Church observed an annual ''Fanny Crosby Day'' in her honor. Her influence has had a broad reach.

The real turning point in Fanny Crosby's life came when she was accepted as a student, just before her fifteenth birthday, at the trend-setting New York Institution for the Blind—in those days the best such school in the nation. It was so new when Fanny was accepted that she was the thirty-first student enrolled.

She excelled there in her eight years as a student (she would teach at the institution for another fifteen years) and it was there that she began to write verse as a vocation. Few took her efforts at poetry seriously until a guest at the school, celebrated phrenologist George Combe, studied the conformation of her skull and decreed that she was meant to be a *famous* poetess. She believed it and, given the community standing of the source of the prediction, so did everyone else.

It was an era in which the education of the blind was being heavily promoted, based on Frenchman Louis Braille's system of writing for the blind that uses characters made up of raised dots. He had first published it in 1826 and refined it five years later. The growing availability of schoolbooks in Braille led to more and more schools for the blind, encouraged by the success of the New York school.

In 1842, the New York Institution for the Blind took twenty of its most promising students "on the road," touring them on the Hudson River by canalboat, making platform appearances in towns along the way. Fanny, reciting her own poetry, was a featured performer.

In the autumn of 1843, a party from the school went to Washington to appear before the United States Congress. Fanny, writing in her *Memories of Eighty Years,* remembered the fear she felt about appearing before such an august body: ". . . the inspiration of the hour was sufficient to fortify me against . . . dreaded failure. At any rate I tried to do my level best; and when I finished my poem there was a dreadful silence which I interpreted to mean that the audience was not pleased. With mingled emotions, alternating between hope and fear, I waited, it seemed to me, as long as five minutes; in reality I suppose, not more than thirty seconds passed before there was such a tremendous applause that I was actually frightened.''

Applause continued until Fanny agreed to recite an encore poem.

In 1844, her first volume of poetry, *The Blind Girl and Other Poems,* was published. Her verse was also being published in the *New York Herald,* the *Saturday Evening Post,* and the *Fireman's Journal,* a weekly publication of New York City's volunteer fire companies.

Then, in April of 1847, Fannie again appeared before Congress with a group from the institution. ''During our stay in Washington,'' she recalled, ''we had the privilege of hearing the last speech of John Quincy Adams. The audience was so still that the faintest noise in any part of the room seemed to be very loud, and we waited breathlessly to hear what the aged statesman would say to the rising generation. His voice had lost much of its original sweetness and power but it fell upon our ears with a strange cadence that echoed in my memory for many years after the voice itself had ceased to be a great and commanding force in the councils of the nation.''

That trip to Washington also included a White House audience with President James K. Polk, with Miss Crosby singing a song she had composed as a dedication to the chief executive.

The work of the New York Institution for the Blind had become so important in the pre-Civil War era that few men in the public eye could ignore its presence. Pilgrimages to the building at Thirty-ninth Street and Ninth Avenue, ''in the midst of a delightful suburban district in plain view of the Hudson River,'' became commonplace for the great and near-great. Thus, Fanny and her fellow students met the likes of Horace Greeley and Henry Clay and William Cullen Bryant and, importantly, Grover Cleveland.

The future president's brother, William, was the head teacher at the school for the blind; young Grover joined the staff as assistant to the superintendent. For more than a year he worked with Fanny, taking dictation from her and copying down her poems.

Fanny Crosby was fortunate, too, that her days at the institution coincided with what one observer of the era has called "the golden age of the gospel song." And, it must be added, Fanny was also fortunate to become associated with two disciples of Dr. Lowell Mason, justly called the "father of American church music." Mason (1792–1872) promoted elementary musical education in the churches, the teaching of music in the public schools, and the popularization of classical chorus singing. It was in 1845 that George F. Root, one of Mason's teachers and choir singers, joined the staff of the school for the blind to teach vocal training.

Root was already well known as a composer of hymns and "secular pieces," and he took Fanny under his wing, using her as a sounding board for his many melodies. It seemed inevitable that they would become collaborators.

The first was titled "Fare Thee Well, Kitty Dear," which, in Fanny's recollection, "described the grief of a colored man on the death of his beloved." It was stilted and it was clear that Fanny had no idea at all as to what was the patois of an 1840s black man. The chorus ran like this:

> *Fare thee well, Kitty dear,*
> *Thou art sleeping in thy grave so low,*
> *Nevermore, Kitty dear,*
> *Wilt thou listen to my old banjo.*

In a three-year period, then, the Crosby-Root collaboration accounted for some fifty to sixty songs, with such titles as "Bird of the North," "Hazel Dell," "They Have Sold Me Down the River," "Rosalie, the Prairie Flower," "There's Music in the Air," "Never Forget the Dear Ones," and "Proud World, Good-bye, I'm Going Home."

In 1858 (Fanny was thirty-eight) she left the institution to marry Alexander Van Alstyne, also blind, whom she had known as a pupil and a teacher in the school for fifteen years. After their marriage, he insisted that she continue to publish under her own name—a rare liberal attitude for a husband in the middle 1800s. They made their home in Brooklyn and had one child, who died in infancy. Oddly, even though they collaborated on a few hymns and she occasionally used "Mrs. Van Alstyne" as one of her pseudonyms, she wrote very little about him (only a passing paragraph or two) in either of her autobiographies: *Fanny Crosby's Life-Story by Herself* (1903) and *Memories of Eighty Years* (1906). Van Alstyne had died in 1902.

Her full-time career as a writer of gospel lyrics began in February of 1864 (she was almost forty-four), when she met with William B. Bradbury, another devotee of Dr. Lowell Mason and, by that time, a successful music publisher who was regarded as the "father" of popular Sunday school music. He was aware of her poetry and her collaboration with George Root and told her he believed she could write hymns, encouraging her to do so.

Three days later she returned to his office with a four-stanza lyric, which he set to music and published. It was hardly great poetry but it was "singable":

> *We are going, we are going*
> *To a home beyond the skies,*

Where the fields are robed in beauty
And the sunlight never dies . . .

Within a week after getting that lyric Bradbury sent for Fanny and said he needed a patriotic song at once; the Civil War was winding down and the tides had turned for the Union. He had chosen "A Sound Among the Mulberry Trees" for a title. Somewhat timidly she suggested that "Forest Trees" would be more euphonious and Bradbury agreed. The melody he had composed was somewhat difficult, but the following morning she was back in his office with the completed lyrics.

Bradbury made her a promise: "As long as I have a publishing house, you will have work." He died in January of 1868, but Fanny would stay with the successor company to Bradbury's, the Biglow and Main Company, for more than forty years. One of the partners in the latter company was Sylvester Main, who had been a childhood chum.

"The most enduring hymns," Fanny would say, "are born in the silences of the soul." Whatever the truth of that, she could work fast as well as work long hours. So prolific was she, writing with at least twenty different composers, that her publishers were reluctant to credit her directly with all she wrote. Thus came the long list of pseudonyms and initials, including the likes of James Apple, Rose Atherton, James Black, Henrietta E. Blair, Florence Booth, Charles Bruce, Leah Carlton, Lyman Cuyler, Ella Dale, Rian J. Dykes, Lizzie Edwards, Grace J. Frances, Victoria Frances, Jennie Garnet, Mrs. Kate Grinley, Ruth Harmon, Frances Hope, Martha J. Lankton, W. Robert Lindsay, Allie Martin, Alice Monteith, Victoria Sterling, Zemira Wallace, and on and on. And sometimes just "Fanny" or "FJC" and sometimes just "F."

When one writes nine thousand lyrics or more, the

music critics can be expected to carp a bit. John Julian in his *Dictionary of Hymnology,* accepted as the standard work in the field, said of her work: "Mrs. Van Alstyne's hymns . . . are with few exceptions very weak and poor, their simplicity and earnestness being their redeeming features." Critic S. A. W. Duffield wrote: "It is more to Mrs. Van Alstyne's credit that she has occasionally found a pearl than that she has brought to the surface so many oyster shells."

To churchgoers, though, there have been a great many Fanny Crosby pearls. Indeed, that very simplicity and earnestness of her words, with their easily remembered recurrent phrases, is what has endeared them to singers—yesterday and today. The fact that Fanny's gospel songs say what the worshippers themselves *want* to say is what has made them last.

In writing her two autobiographies, Fanny recognized what was the best she had done, giving little space to the "oyster shells." The stories she tells about writing specific hymns single out the Crosby "hits."

Fanny remembered that her favorite collaborator, William Howard Doane—they wrote 1,500 hymns together—came to her on April 30, 1868, and said to her: " 'I have exactly forty minutes before my train leaves for Cincinnati. Here is the melody. Can you write words for it?'

"I replied that I would see what I can do. Then followed a period of twenty minutes during which I was unconscious of all else except the work I was doing. At the end of that time I recited the words to 'Safe in the Arms of Jesus.' Mr. Doane copied them down and had time to catch his train."

In those twenty minutes, Fanny had written three long stanzas and a chorus. True, they were seeded with the repetitiveness that often marks her work but this time she had created a pearl. It was to become one of her most lasting and beloved hymns:

> *Safe in the arms of Jesus,*
> *Safe on His gentle breast,*
> *There by His love o'ershaded,*
> *Sweetly my soul shall rest.*

There was a somewhat similar experience with "Blessed Assurance" written "to a melody composed by my friend, Mrs. Joseph F. Knabb. She played it over once or twice on the piano and then asked me what it said to me. I replied,

> *'Blessed assurance, Jesus is mine,*
> *O what a foretaste of glory divine!*
> *Heir of salvation, purchase of God,*
> *Born of His spirit, washed in His blood:*
> *Praising my Saviour all the day long.' "*

The quickness of Fanny's mind and her ability to remember lyrics as she was "writing" them came precisely because she was blind; she had adapted to the reality that she could not just jot down a note to remind her of a phrase or a line of a song. Memorization was a *must*. Then, too, there was the redundancy of certain phrases in American gospel songs; "hymnspeak," you might say. And Fanny's facile brain had a huge file of them.

Very often a composer would just provide her with a tentative title and she would flesh out—from her own experiences, observations and mental file—the full lyrics. That's the way it was when collaborator William Doane sent her the title "Rescue the Perishing." Several days later, Fanny was doing work at a mission on New York's Bowery when a young man came forward with a sad story about being alienated from his dying mother. There were prayers said for him.

"And while I sat there that evening," Fanny wrote, "the line came to me: *Rescue the perishing, care for the dying.* I could think of nothing else that night. When I arrived at my home I went to work on it at once; and before I retired the entire hymn was ready for a melody. The next day my words were written and forwarded to Mr. Doane, who wrote the beautiful and touching music as it now stands."

> *Rescue the perishing, care for the dying,*
> *Snatch them in pity from sin and the grave;*
> *Weep o'er the erring one, lift up the fallen,*
> *Tell them of Jesus the mighty to save.*

The Crosby-Doane collaboration would turn out more of those gospel "hits" than any other songwriting team of the era. And it was vastly important to Fanny's fiscal well-being because Doane was the leading publisher of songbooks for the burgeoning Sunday school market. His first book, *Sabbath School Gems,* was published in 1862, followed in 1864 by *Little Sunbeams.* Then, in 1867, Doane published his most popular Sunday school music book: *Silver Spray.* A year later he followed with *Songs of Devotion,* an adult hymnal for church. All included Fanny Crosby songs, which were also some of Doane's best compositions:

> *Draw me nearer, nearer, nearer blessed Lord,*
> *To the cross where Thou has died;*
> *Draw me nearer, nearer, nearer blessed Lord,*
> *To Thy precious bleeding side.*

> *Pass me not, O gentle Saviour,*
> *Hear my humble cry,*

While on others Thou are calling,
Do not pass me by.

In the cross, in the cross,
Be my glory ever;
Till my raptured soul shall find,
Rest beyond the river.

Fanny was able to work with the best hymn publishers and composers of her time. In addition to Doane, the most prolific partners were Philip Phillips, successful publisher of Sunday school singing books and a superb concert singer (525 collaborations); the Reverend Dr. Robert Lowry, composer and Sunday school songbook editor for Biglow & Main, Fanny's publisher (219); and Ira D. Sankey (237), the great song leader for the immensely popular evangelist Dwight L. Moody.

"Most of my poems," Fanny wrote, "have been written during the long night watches, when the distractions of the day could not interfere with the rapid flow of thought. . . . But I never have any portion of a poem committed to paper until the entire poem is composed."

She recalled how she worked with collaborator Philip Phillips: "In 1866, Mr. Phillips published a collection of hymns called *The Singing Pilgrim*; and while he was preparing that book he sent me forty titles to which I composed words and not a single poem was written [down] by my amanuensis until the whole number was completed. They were then forwarded to Mr. Phillips at Cincinnati; he again sent me a long list of titles and they were treated exactly as the first forty had been.

"This incident is not told to commend myself, but merely to illustrate to what extent memory will serve us, if we only give memory a fair chance. The mind appears to me like a great storehouse into which we place various articles for safe keeping and sometimes even forget that they are there, but, sooner or later, we find them; and so I lay aside my intellectual wares for some future day of need; and in the meantime often forget them, until the call comes for a hymn.''

But even Fanny Crosby's incredible powers of memorization sometimes failed her. There was one occasion when she attended a Moody-Sankey evangelistic meeting and heard the audience sing ''O My Saviour, Hide Me,'' a song with which she was much pleased. As she related the incident:

''Turning to Mr. Sankey, I asked, 'Where did you get that piece?' He paid no attention to my question, for he supposed I was merely joking; and at that moment the bell called us to dinner—so both of us forgot about the hymn. But it was used again at the afternoon service; and then I was determined to know who wrote it.

'' 'Mr. Sankey,' I said, 'now you must tell me who is the author of ''O My Saviour, Hide Me.'' '

'' 'Really,' he replied, 'don't you recall who wrote that hymn? You ought to remember, for you are the guilty one.' ''

Any summing up of Frances Jane Crosby Van Alstyne must deal with the reality that she created a public persona that was almost impossible to maintain. She characterized herself as ''the restless Fanny Crosby,'' projecting a self-assured, unafraid individual, one capable of succeeding against all adversity.

Yet during all of her long life she was dependent on others: those who had to travel with her to be her eyes, those who copied down her poems and hymn lyrics and book texts. In all candor, she was a dependent individual with pride enough to deny it.

Only in her hymn writing did she acknowledge a dependency, most especially with the gospel hymn she wrote in 1880 with old friend Hubert P. Main: ''Hold Thou My Hand.'' Here she used one of her pseudonyms, Grace J. Frances, most likely because she didn't want the name of Fanny Crosby associated with lyrics that clearly had a blind person's connotation. Also there's a despondency in the words that was contrary to Fanny's constantly upbeat public personality:

Hold Thou my hand, so weak I am and helpless,
I dare not take one step without Thy aid;
Hold Thou my hand, for then, O living Saviour,
No dread of ill shall make my soul afraid.

Hold Thou my hand, till, all my journey over,
I see the gates of Edenland so fair;
Hold Thou my hand, O do not, do not leave me,
Hold Thou my hand till I am safely there.

If ''Hold Thou My Hand'' can be said to mirror a certain vulnerability in Fanny, it can also be argued that it was yet another reaffirmation of her unquenchable faith.

Sometime later, a visiting Scottish minister commented on her blindness, lamenting the fact that God had not blessed her with sight.

Her reaction was immediate: ''Do you know that, if at birth I had been able to make one petition to my Creator, it would have been that I should be born blind?''

''Why?'' asked the startled clergyman.

''Because, when I get to heaven, the first face that shall gladden my sight will be that of my Saviour!''

No one who ever knew Fanny Crosby, or who had sung her hymns, could doubt the faith behind that statement; it was a faith repeated again and again in some nine thousand gospel songs.

She would die on the morning of February 12, 1915, just a few days shy of her ninety-fifth birthday. At nine o'clock on the preceding evening she had dictated a letter of comfort to a bereaved friend. And then she went to sleep, quietly, without illness or loss of faculties, never to wake again.

Her funeral at Bridgeport, Connecticut, was said to be the largest in that city up to that time. And those attending heard the reading of a eulogistic poem sent by Eliza E. Hewitt of Philadelphia, another well-known hymn lyricist:

> *Good-bye, dearest Fanny, good-bye for a while;*
> *You walk in the shadows no more;*
> *Around you the sunbeams of glory will smile;*
> *The Lamb is the light of that shore!*
>
> *Some day we will meet in the City above;*
> *Together we'll look on His face;*
> *Safe, "Safe in the Arms of Jesus" we love,*
> *Together we'll sing "Saved By Grace."*

A small stone marking her final resting place is engraved with a simple message:

AUNT FANNY,

FANNY J. CROSBY.

SHE HATH DONE WHAT SHE COULD.

2

Ira D. Sankey

GOSPEL MUSIC . . .

That generic term can best be attributed to one man—Ira David Sankey, perhaps the most outstanding evangelistic song leader in American history. It should be noted that Sankey coined the term with a compilation of a series of nineteenth-century songbooks titled *Gospel Hymns.* It marked the first time that the word "gospel" (from the Anglo-Saxon "godspel," meaning "glad tidings") was used in association with Christian music. Thus, *gospel music.*

But that's getting ahead of the story.

Sankey was born in the village of Edenberg, Mercer County (later Lawrence County), western Pennsylvania, on August 28, 1840, into a Scotch-Irish family prominent in the state's early political history, the Revolutionary War, and the War of 1812. And born, too, into a family where music and the Methodist church were both of paramount importance. Ira learned to read music and play the piano and organ at an early age. His was a happy childhood; his family was well-to-do, if not wealthy. In 1857, his father, David, was made president of the Bank of New Castle, Pennsylvania, in which Ira, after attending high school, became a clerk.

In New Castle, the young man joined the Methodist church and was soon chosen choir leader as well as superintendent of the Sunday school. Those were troubled times in the nation; when the Civil War broke out Sankey enlisted in the Union army—in Company B of the 22nd Regiment of Pennsylvania Volunteers, a three-month enlistment group.

That military unit was stationed in Maryland, ill equipped and ill prepared for battle. At religious services in tents and around campfires Ira began to lead the singing. He organized a choir of soldiers and helped out at local Maryland church functions as a song leader.

When Sankey's one-term enlistment ended (he saw no fighting) he returned to New Castle to once more work with his father, who had been appointed Collector of Internal Revenue for the 24th Congressional District. In 1863 he married Fannie V. Edwards, a member of his church choir and a daughter of State Senator John Edwards. He had settled into a comfortable middle class, small town life-style.

Then, in 1870, his entire world changed.

Ira was appointed by the New Castle Young Men's Christian Association as a delegate to the international convention of the YMCA in Indianapolis. The story is told that at a convention prayer meeting, a fellow Pennsylvania delegate, the Reverend Robert McMillan, said to him: "Mr. Sankey, the singing here has been abominable. I wish you would start up something when that man stops praying, if he ever does."

When the opportunity finally came, Sankey rose and began a familiar hymn, "There is a Fountain Filled with Blood," in which the delegates joined heartily. At the close of the service, Reverend McMillan introduced Ira to the Chicago YMCA delegate, Dwight L. Moody. Sankey would write later of that encounter:

"As I drew near Mr. Moody he stepped forward, and, taking me by the hand, looked at me in that keen, piercing fashion of his, as if reading my very soul. Then he said abruptly, 'Where are you from?'

" 'Pennsylvania,' I replied.

" 'Are you married?'

" 'I am.'

" 'How many children have you?'

" 'Two.'

" 'What is your business?'

" 'I am a government officer.'

" 'Well, you'll have to give it up!'

"I was much too astonished to make any reply, and he went on, as if the matter had already been decided: 'I have been looking for you for the last eight years. You'll have to come to Chicago and help me in my work.' "

Moody, three years Sankey's senior, had been born of Puritan stock in East Northfield, Massachusetts (February 5, 1837). His father had died when he was only four and the young Dwight was a mischievous, independent boy who got little formal schooling. At seventeen, he became a salesman in a relative's shoe store in Boston, displaying an obvious natural talent for selling. A year later he was "converted" by a Sunday school teacher. Pledging himself to Christ was a serious challenge to him and in 1856, then only nineteen, he took that challenge to Chicago. On the streets of that bustling, raw midwestern city he was to become a missionary—with no formal schooling and little money.

What Dwight Lyman Moody had was an inexhaustible energy for the work of his Lord; an unshakable belief that God would provide, no matter what. He put together a Sunday school class from among the young toughs of the Chicago streets—with colorful names like Darby the Cobbler, Billy Bucktooth, and Madden the Butcher—and eventually opened what was known as the North Market Sabbath School. Before long the "school" was ministering to nearly a thousand repentant hoodlums and had reached the status of a Chicago institution. So much so that the North Market Sabbath School and its evangelistic leader were visited by President-elect Abraham Lincoln.

The Civil War saw Moody going to the front as an agent of the Christian Commission, a volunteer group designed to help the small corps of army chaplains and provide Christian solace for the soldiers. After the war, it was back to Chicago where Moody's reputation grew. He was an outstanding fund-raiser for all kinds of Christian work: missions, churches, Sunday schools. And he wanted to do more. One newspaper called him "the lightning Christian of the lightning city."

Then came the year 1870, the YMCA national convention in Indianapolis, and Moody's invitation to Sankey. Ira hesitated for several months but, after much urging on Moody's part, he consented to spend a week with him in Chicago. Before the week was out he resigned his Internal Revenue position and joined forces with Moody. That was early in 1871 and Sankey was quickly involved in Moody's work: speaking and singing at daily noon prayer meetings, singing and praying with the sick, and whatever else Moody asked of him in the inner-city missionary work.

But on October 8, 1871, it all seemed to come to an end in the Great Chicago Fire. Moody and Sankey were conducting a meeting in Farwell Hall, where the evangelist had both his living quarters and his office. The place was crowded to the doors. When Moody had finished his sermon Sankey started a meeting-closing solo,

"Today the Saviour Calls." Before he could finish his voice was drowned out by the noise of fire engines rushing past the hall and by the tolling of bells. The meeting was ended abruptly. They could see the reflections of a huge fire only half a mile away.

Then, suddenly, the high winds changed direction, aiming the roaring blaze directly at Farwell Hall. Immediate evacuation became necessary. Sankey removed his personal belongings from the building and eventually found a drayman who, for the exorbitant fee of ten dollars, took him and his baggage to the Fort Wayne and Chicago Railway station, where Ira was able to board an outgoing train heading east and in the direction of his Pennsylvania home.

As for Dwight Moody, he was later to tell a friend, "All I saved was my Bible, my family, and my reputation."

Sankey was sure that his work with Moody had ended in the devastating fire. But two months later he received a telegram from the indefatigable evangelist urging him to return to Chicago, to join him at the temporary "tabernacle" being built. Ira didn't hesitate. This time he moved his family to Chicago, taking charge of the tabernacle work while Moody was making his second evangelistic trip to England. Moody's lightning was striking far beyond Chicago.

It was in June of 1873 that Moody and Sankey made their first trip together to Great Britain. That initial "team" visit started rather quietly in York and they worked hard for five months in the north of England, awakening enough interest there to be invited to Scotland. In Edinburgh they enlisted the support of both the Church of Scotland and the Free Church, two feuding factions joining hands for the first time. It should be noted that Sankey, traveling with a portable reed organ (or harmonium), dispelled the traditional Scottish abhorrence to the use of instrumental music in worship services.

It was during a meeting in Edinburgh that Sankey's skills as a musician came to the fore in a dramatic fashion. Just the day before he had clipped a poem by one Elizabeth C. Clephane from a newspaper; a verse based on Christ's parable of the lost sheep (Matthew 18:10–14). Ira put it among his papers for possible future use. On the very next day, after Moody had finished a sermon titled "The Good Shepherd," he turned to Sankey and asked him to "sing a solo appropriate for this subject."

"I had nothing suitable in mind," Sankey would reveal later in his memoirs, "and was greatly troubled what to do. The Twenty-third Psalm occurred to me, but this had been sung several times in the meeting. . . . At this moment, I seemed to hear a voice saying, 'Sing the hymn you found [in the newspaper].' But I thought this impossible as no music had ever been written. Again the impression came strongly upon me that I must sing the beautiful and appropriate words I had found the day before, and placing the little newspaper slip on the organ in front of me, I lifted my heart in prayer, asking God to help me so to sing that the people might hear and understand. Laying my hands upon the organ, I struck the key of A flat, and began to sing . . ."

> *There were ninety and nine that safely lay*
> *In the shelter of the fold.*
> *But one was out on the hills away,*
> *Far off from the gates of gold—*
> *Away on the mountains wild and bare,*
> *Away from the tender Shepherd's care,*
> *Away from the tender Shepherd's care.*

"Lord, Thou has here Thy ninety and nine,
Are they not enough for Thee?"
But the Shepherd made answer: "This of mine
Has wandered away from me.
And although the road be rough and steep,
I go to the desert to find my sheep,
I go to the desert to find my sheep."

"Note by note the tune was given," Sankey recalled, "which has not been changed from that day . . ."

But none of the ransomed ever knew
How deep were the waters crossed;
Nor how dark was the night that the Lord
    passed through
'Ere He found His sheep that was lost.
Out in the desert He heard its cry—
Sick and helpless, and ready to die,
Sick and helpless, and ready to die.

"Lord, whence are those blood-drops all the way
That mark out the mountains' track?"
"They were shed for the one who had gone astray,
'Ere the Shepherd could bring him back."
"Lord, whence are Thy hands so rent and torn?"
"They're pierced tonight by many a thorn,
They're pierced tonight by many a thorn."

But all through the mountains, thunder-riv'n,
And up from the rocky steep,
There arose a glad cry to the gate of heaven,
"Rejoice, I have found my sheep!"
And the angels echoed around the throne,
"Rejoice, for the Lord brings back His own!
Rejoice, for the Lord brings back His own."

"As the singing ceased," Ira wrote, "a great sigh seemed to go up from the meeting, and I knew that the song had reached the hearts of my Scotch audience. Mr. Moody was dearly moved. Leaving the pulpit, he came down to where I was seated. Leaning over the organ, he looked at the little newspaper slip from which the song had been sung and with tears in his eyes, said, 'Sankey . . . I never heard the like of it in my life.'"

Moody, who did not sing himself, fully recognized the impact of music in Christian worship. He said: "I feel sure the great majority do like singing. It helps to build an audience—even if you do preach a dry sermon. If you have singing that reaches the heart, it will fill the church every time. There is more said in the Bible about praise than prayer, and music and song have not only accompanied all Scripture revivals, but are essential in deepening spiritual life. Singing does at least as much as preaching to impress the word of God upon people's minds. Ever since God first called me, the importance of praise expressed in song has grown upon me."

And on that summer 1873 day in Edinburgh, Dwight Moody knew for certain that he had chosen exactly the right music man for his evangelistic meetings. He had witnessed, firsthand, the power of the impact of "The Ninety and Nine," with its divinely inspired composition.

After Edinburgh came Glasgow and four months in other Scottish cities. Ireland was next, where they were welcomed in both Belfast and Dublin. Then back to England: Manchester, Sheffield, Birmingham, and, finally, London. In London, they conducted 285 meetings, in numerous halls, attended by 2,530,000 people.

The Moody-Sankey revival meetings attracted heavy coverage in the British press, some of it carping but

most of it laudatory, serving to increase the size of the
audiences. His Royal Highness, the Prince of Wales,
came, as did other lesser members of the royal family;
Queen Victoria, as head of the Church of England, de-
clined an invitation to be present.

In August of 1875, the two evangelists returned to
the United States in triumph. They undertook an unbe-
lievably difficult schedule of revival meetings across
America: filling New York City's Hippodrome each
night for two months, doing the same in the cavernous
freight depot of the Pennsylvania Railroad in Philadelphia, with President Ulysses S. Grant in attendance on
one night, and continuing on with revival meetings in
Brooklyn, Boston, Baltimore, St. Louis, Kansas City,
Nashville, Louisville, San Francisco—few major cities
in the United States were without a Moody-Sankey
revival.

There also followed two other protracted visits to the
British Isles—in 1881 to 1883 and again in 1891 to
1892. Once more millions heard the messages and sang
the songs.

In 1893, as just one more example of their appeal,
they rented a "big top" tent from the Forepaugh Circus
for a Sunday morning service during the Chicago
World's Fair. Eighteen thousand attended! The drawing
power of the revivals was not lost on the circus owners;
they asked Moody to provide an evangelist to travel
with the circus as a regular attraction. The offer was
turned aside.

It must not be supposed that Moody and Sankey were
alone in evangelizing America. On the contrary—there
were evangelists of every stripe and ability. It's just
that the Moody-Sankey team may have been better or-
ganizationally and, certainly, Sankey's music distin-
guished their revival meetings.

If there could be considered to be a "rival" to Moody-Sankey's prominence it was a preacher from the hill country of northern Georgia named Samuel Porter Jones; he wanted to be known only as Sam Jones.

Jones had a desire to be a lawyer but he had become an alcoholic. In 1872 his life was turned around when he made a promise to his father, who was on his death-bed, that he would stop drinking. The promise made, and kept, Sam turned to the ministry. For eight years he was a Methodist circuit rider in the poorest rural counties of Georgia. He would write later that he began as a minister with "a wife and one child, a bobtail pony, and eight dollars of cash."

Reverend Jones, though, had a gift. He could stir an audience like few other preachers. He began to build a reputation as a fiery evangelist, one with the common touch. "God projected this world on a 'root hog or die poor' principle," he would tell his audiences. "If the hog, or man either, don't root, let him die."

But he was essentially a happy man: "Fun is the next best thing to religion. When I get up to preach, I just knock out the bung and let nature cut her capers."

In April of 1885 a group of church leaders in Nashville called on Pastor Jones to conduct a three-week series of revivals meetings in the city. He wanted a tent or auditorium that would seat three thousand; better yet, five thousand. What he got was a huge tent seating eight thousand, erected on a lot on Broad Street. And when he began preaching on Sunday afternoon, May 2, 1885, the seats were filled and two thousand more stood around outside the canvas.

The evangelist began a series of four services a day: one at sunrise, another at 10:00 a.m. one in the afternoon, and then again in the evening. He railed against worldliness, drunkenness, gambling, and any manner of sin he found around him.

Into this charged atmosphere came Captain Tom
Ryman, the wealthy owner of a fleet of "pleasure"
boats plying the Cumberland River—boats dedicated to
dancing, gambling, and drinking. It is part of the lore
of Nashville that Captain Tom and members of his
rowdy crew went to the tent revival services determined
to disrupt them. They meant to make sport of Pastor
Sam Jones.

The Reverend Mr. Jones was equal to the challenge.
In the course of that evening's services, and during a
stunning peroration on the subject of motherhood, the
rough Tom Ryman was brought to his knees, converted
to Christ. It is said that Captain Ryman led his crewmen
back to the boats to throw gaming tables and teakwood
bars overboard.

Whatever the exact truth of that part of the story,
Ryman *had* converted and he vowed to build Jones a
tabernacle so "that Sam Jones will never have to preach
in a tent again." He did just that, erecting an edifice
of brick and mortar in downtown Nashville to be called
the Union Gospel Tabernacle. It would later become
the Ryman Auditorium, posthumously honoring Captain
Tom, and even later (in the early 1940s) it would become the Grand Ole Opry House, the "Mother Church
of Country Music."

But what was most important about that three-week
revival program in Nashville was that it made Sam
Jones a national figure and he began to get invitations
from Northern cities. To accept them he realized that
he needed the presence of more music; that he needed
to counter Dwight Moody's Ira Sankey. And so Pastor
Jones hired a robust six-foot Chicagoan named E. O.
(Edwin Othello) Excell—like Sankey, he was a native
of western Pennsylvania.

Excell was a gospel songwriter, an author of Sunday
school books, and a singing evangelist so full of music

he seemed to have "swallowed a brass band," according to one newspaper account. There was no doubt that Excell, with his "full, round baritone of great volume," was more of a showman than was Ira Sankey. And there was no doubt, either, that both Moody and Jones held major revival meetings in the same cities, more than a few times back-to-back.

However, it was less of a competitive situation between evangelists than it was a manifestation of the broad public acceptance of a revivalist Christian religion in the post-Civil War decades of the nineteenth century. There was a great demand for more revival meetings; the demand was filled.

But in the context of telling the story of Ira Sankey, perhaps the most important aspect of the Moody-Sankey partnership was the phenomenon of the songbooks. Published collections of the songs used in the Moody-Sankey meetings (many written by Sankey) were popular worldwide. The first was *Sacred Songs and Solos,* published initially in London in 1873. Eventually, eight million copies were sold. So pervading, so popular, were the songs chosen for that publication that even today, in England and in mission fields around the globe, gospel-type songs are known as "Sankeys."

Sankey joined with Philip Paul Bliss, another western Pennsylvania native and a prolific writer ("Let the Lower Lights Be Burning" is one of his), to compile a series of songbooks under the blanket title of *Gospel Hymns.* Sankey and Bliss published volumes one and two in 1875 and 1876. Then in late December of 1876, Bliss and his wife were killed in a train wreck in Ashtabula, Ohio. Sankey finished the other four volumes, the last in 1891.

Many of the songs in the *Gospel Hymns* series are still widely used (and are found in present-day hymnals): "Hiding In Thee," "I'm Praying for You," "Faith is the Victory," "The Ninety and Nine," "The Story That Never Grows Old," "Believe and Obey," among them.

The messages of those songs are direct and completely understandable. An example is "Believe and Obey," with lyrics by Julia Sterling and music by Ira Sankey:

> *Believe and obey, believe and obey,*
> *The Master is calling, no longer delay;*
> *The light of His mercy shines bright on the way*
> *Of all who confess him—believe and obey.*

Had Sankey and Moody chosen to personally profit from those songbooks they both would have been wealthy men. Instead, *all* royalties on the millions upon millions of songbooks sold were turned over to a board of trustees; most of the money was used to support two Christian schools Moody had founded in Northfield, Massachusetts: Northfield Seminary for Girls and Mount Hermon School for Boys.

Sankey was able to use some of the money to have a new YMCA building erected in New Castle, Pennsylvania, the dedication of it highlighted by Sankey himself leading in the singing of hymns.

Without Moody, who was ill, Sankey undertook a crusade of his own to the Holy Land in 1898, a moving experience for him. He travelled over the road Jesus had travelled on His way to Calvary. And Ira was able to sing at the Tower of David while in Jerusalem.

Dwight Moody died in 1899. Perhaps his greatest legacy was the founding of the Chicago (today, Moody) Bible Institute, where thousands of Christian workers have been trained in Bible study and in practical methods of social reform.

The Moody-Sankey collaboration would set the standards for Christian crusade teams of the twentieth century. They were very much alike. Both were big men and both were characterized by contemporary writers as having a "sweetness" of spirit that marked their work. Moody's sermons were colloquial, simple, and full of conviction. So, too, were Sankey's songs. Perhaps they were men predestined to meet and to work together in a noble cause.

Sadly, Ira Sankey's last years were spent in blindness in his home in Brooklyn, New York, where he died on August 13, 1908, just fifteen days before his sixty-eighth birthday. The Associated Press report on his death said: ". . . Sankey wrote the gospel hymns of the world. In China, Egypt, India, Japan, in almost every language known to man, his hymns were sung. His voice was . . . clear, strong, thrilling. His own emotion vibrated through every note and set the hearts of his hearers to throbbing in unison. Never was a burning zeal put into more contagious and persuasive notes."

On August 28, 1940, New Castle, Pennsylvania, observed the centenary of Sankey's birth. A highlight was the gift from the Moody family to the citizens of New Castle of an Estey organ that Sankey had played for many years during the Moody revival meetings.

An epitaph?

One contemporary said that Moody with his messages and Sankey with his songs had "reduced the population of Hell by a million souls."

3

Homer Rodeheaver

Ⅱ HOMER RODEHEAVER'S ROLE IN GOSPEL MUSIC COULD be expressed in a single word—an admittedly difficult task—that word would have to be "entrepreneur." Because in addition to serving as a noted song leader in worldwide evangelism for most of his adult life, Rodeheaver was the first to establish a privately owned music publishing company specifically for gospel music and the first to put into being a record label solely for sacred music performers.

Thus, if "entrepreneur" is defined as one who organizes, manages, and assumes the risks of a business or enterprise, it also defines the colorful career of Ohio-born and Tennessee-nurtured Homer Alvan Rodeheaver.

Without meaning to be judgmental, it can be said that Rodeheaver clearly understood that evangelism and the music born of it was big business.

Very little of his early life seemed to presage his future. He was born on October 4, 1880, the third son of Thurman and Fannie (Armstrong) Rodeheaver, on a small isolated farm near the village of Union Furnace, Ohio. When Homer was only a year old, the family moved to Newcomb, Tennessee, hard by the Kentucky border, where Thurman Rodeheaver started a lumber business. Later, son Homer would recall his parents as a "Godly mother and a rugged Christian father."

The mother died when Homer was eight years old; the father would remarry. The children of both marriages—there were five in all—were raised as Methodists. Author Basil Miller in his *Ten Singers Who Became Famous* wrote that "during his Tennessee days, Homer attended camp meetings with the family, and under the influence of a sermon [at one of them] he went forward and yielded himself to God."

Hard work and an on-and-off education dominated his early years. His father gave him a mule team, which he drove to haul logs and lumber to the family mill and to the railroad. Later he also hauled coal from an uncle's mine to the tip-house. The routine was that he worked six months out of a year and went to school during the other six.

His oldest brother, Yumbert, would recall in a 1921 magazine article: "My parents were not enthusiastic over an extensive education. Their environments did not demand nor require it."

What parental enthusiasm there was centered around the church and its music. Both the father and the mother sang; the eldest son was encouraged to learn to play a small cottage organ. Yumbert Rodeheaver did have a few lessons from a teacher but he was largely self-taught. He learned to play so that he might accompany his father, who led the music for the Methodist Sunday School. And Yumbert passed what he knew about music along to the younger Homer.

First, he taught Homer how to properly keep the musical beat on a bass drum. That learned, Homer bought a cornet and taught himself to play it.

It was with brother Yumbert that Homer had his first away-from-home adventure. Together, they enlisted in the army in 1898 during the Spanish-American War. They served in the Fourth Tennessee Regimental Band and were sent to Cuba just as the war ended. In four boring months of garrison duty on the island the brothers, as Yumbert recalled it, had no "enemies to fight [but] the Cuban flies and tarantulas."

On returning home, Homer was encouraged by another brother, Joseph, to get a year of high school training so that he might enroll at the Methodist Ohio Wesleyan University at Delaware, Ohio (obviously, college entry requirements were less demanding in those days). College records show that he enrolled in September of 1902 and left in June of 1903.

And what did Homer Rodeheaver do at Ohio Wesleyan? For one thing, he was a cheerleader. And as a cheerleader, he was hired by a local pastor as a song leader; it wasn't that he had such a great voice, but he was adept at leading a crowd. For another thing, it was at Ohio Wesleyan that he played in the band, acquiring a slide trombone. In a strange way, that nonacademic college experience set the pattern for the rest of his life.

Somehow—and it is not clear just how—young Homer Rodeheaver came to the attention of the Reverend William B. Biederwolf, who asked him to lead the music for one of the Biederwolf evangelistic campaigns. It was to be a temporary job spanning two weeks. But their association lasted five years, from 1904 to 1909. Rodeheaver had found his calling.

In 1909, when he was twenty-nine years old, Homer met the charismatic evangelist Billy Sunday, a former good-field–no-hit major league baseball player with the storied Chicago White Stockings of Albert G. Spalding.

Author William G. McLoughlin, Jr. summed up Rodeheaver at the time of that meeting: "[He] possessed a soothing baritone voice, an ingratiating personality, a vaguely handsome face, dark wavy hair, and the stage presence of a veteran trouper. He also had considerable skills as a trombonist, was able to give evangelistic talks, had a knowledge of magic which helped him conduct children's meetings, knew how to direct a large choir, and, above all, had developed the smiling, affable sociability of the professional chorister . . ."

At the time of the Sunday-Rodeheaver meeting and the beginning of their association (approved of by the Reverend Biederwolf), Billy Sunday was certainly a star in the evangelistic firmament. He was not a trained minister and never professed to be: "I know as much about theology as a jackrabbit does about ping-pong." He was a nonstop fighter against sin and he truly wanted to save souls, as his soul had been saved when he fell in love with a girl from the Jefferson Park Presbyterian Christian Endeavor and renounced his drunken, blasphemous days as a ball player.

As a revival preacher, no one had seen the equal of Billy Sunday. He was an unrestrained fireball on the stage. As one contemporary commentator had written: "He blew in from the Middle West like a twister."

"Get right with God!" was his constant theme. "The church needs fighting men," he would roar, "not those hog-jowled, weasel-eyed, sponge-columned, mushy-fisted, jelly-spined, pussy-footing, four-flushing, charlotte-russe Christians!"

Night after night he would work himself into a rage against the devil, the sweat pouring off of him as he would remove his coat and vest and tie and roll up his sleeves, while constantly jumping up and down, crouching, shaking his fists, and running back and forth across the stage. More than once he would run the length of the stage, representing a sinner trying to slide into heaven, ending his dash with a perfect hook slide.

Baseball analogies were always a part of his animated sermons: "There are always people sitting in the grandstand and calling the batter a mutt, complaining he can't hit, he's an ice wagon on the bases. O Lord, give us some coaches out of this tabernacle so that people can be brought home to you. Some of them are dying on second and third base. Lord, we don't want that!"

Or: "We put our hands in our pockets, feel for the nickle to put in the collection plate, and then wonder why the world isn't saved. Lord, there are a lot of people who step up to the collection plate and fan!"

He railed, too, against ministers who denounced his type of evangelism: "They tell me a revival is only temporary; so is a bath, but it does you good. Some preachers don't believe in revivals; neither does the devil. A lot of churches don't need an evangelist as much as they need an undertaker."

Participatory evangelism was in Billy Sunday's style. He would frequently leap to the edge of the platform to point an accusing finger at a suspected "boozer," crying out that a man who drinks is a "dirty, low-down, whisky-soaked, beer-guzzling, bull-necked, foul-mouthed hypocrite!"

Sometimes that personal approach would backfire on Sunday, as it did one evening at a meeting in Nashville's Ryman Auditorium. That night he took out after prostitution, calling Nashville's red-light district "the devil's backbone." Two visiting ladies of the evening sat for a time through his denunciations and then got up to leave.

As they walked up the aisle, the evangelist roared,

the finger pointing, "See, there goes two daughters of the devil!"

One of them turned back to Billy, waved coyly, and shouted in reply: "Goodbye, Daddy!"

In writing about Sunday in his book, *Twenty Years with Billy Sunday,* Homer Rodeheaver said: "Of his outstanding characteristics first place must be given to his unreserved consecration to the task of preaching the Gospel, born of the unswerving faith in the infallibility of the Scriptures and belief in God's plan of salvation.... Nor could the matter of physical condition deter him at all. If he was able to stand on his feet in his room, he made his way to the platform. Time and again, against the advice of physicians, he risked illness to keep appointments. As long as I knew him he gave the work of preaching the Gospel every ounce of physical, mental, and spiritual energy he possessed....

"From the moment he stepped on the platform he was like a violin string tuned to the highest pitch."

For nearly two decades, then, Homer Rodeheaver seemed to be a perfect match for Billy Sunday. The young man was devout, a workaholic, a consummate performer—an equal partner with Sunday in bringing sinners to the Lord along the "sawdust trail."

Sunday's revival meetings were usually held in specially built wooden tabernacles; those in smaller cities could seat five to six thousand, in larger cities the seating capacity was between sixteen and twenty thousand. It's interesting to note that the wooden floors of the tabernacles, once thousands of feet were pounding on them, set up a great din. Billy devised a system of dampening the noise by covering the floors with sawdust or shavings. Thus was born the popular phrase of "hitting the sawdust trail," referring to those who came forward to be converted.

In truth, Rodeheaver did a vaudeville turn while he directed the musical portion of the revival meetings. He told jokes, did magic tricks, sang, and made full use of his trademark slide trombone.

He played the instrument well enough but it was also a marvelous prop for him as he strode the stage to prepare the crowds for Billy Sunday. At one point, as he feigned tuning the horn, Homer would warn, "Careful now, this is a Methodist trombone and it sometimes backslides." At other times he would imitate a sour old sinner and use the trombone as a crutch as he hobbled around the stage. Occasionally, he would even hang a local college banner from the slide. And always, as he raised his arms in an exaggerated manner to conduct the singers, the trombone was "alive" in the crook of an elbow.

Then, too, as part of his responsibilities as leader of the "song services," Rodeheaver would bring in brass bands, school cheerleaders, and a stunning array of soloists, duets, and quartets.

"Mr. Sunday loved a song with a lively lilt and rhythm," Rodeheaver wrote in his *Twenty Years With Billy Sunday*. "He didn't care so much for artistic songs. He was a good judge of the kind of song that would be liked eventually and we always respected his judgment. . . . He was constantly warning me not to permit anyone to come to the platform and sing what he called 'sheet music.' He said it always gave him a nervous chill when he saw someone start to the platform unrolling a sheet of music. . . .

"It was our aim to let Mr. Sunday begin his sermon not later than eight o'clock. If the crowd came early we would begin our song service by seven o'clock, or even six-thirty.

"We usually started off with some of the old familiar hymns everybody could sing, then mixed in some of the newer gospel songs, which we would teach the people, interspersing those with a solo, duet, or special numbers by the great choruses. For the offertory I usually played something on the trombone. One of the most popular of all trombone solos was the old hymn [by Fanny Crosby], 'Safe In the Arms of Jesus.' ''

The ''great choruses'' of which Rodeheaver wrote were his specialty. In each city he would gather those choruses from cooperating churches, civic groups, lodges, or musical organizations, rehearse them, and mold them into a professional-sounding unit. Eventually, Rodeheaver would become known as ''The World's Greatest Song Leader,'' an accolade he did not dispute.

Homer discovered soon enough when he joined the Sunday group that a dress code would prevail. ''He [Sunday] gave a great deal of attention to his personal attire,'' Rodeheaver recalled. ''His suits were immaculate and were worn out more by the cleaner and presser than by use; certain neckties must be used with certain suits; shoes must have new heels at the slightest sign of wear; his overcoats and hats presented the appearance of having just arrived from the haberdashery. Gray was his favorite color. . . .

''His interest in sartorial perfection extended to members of his party as well. Often he would call the pianist to his side and whisper: 'Do you think Rody [Rodeheaver] is ever going to get those pants pressed?' . . . Many times he crossed the platform to me and began adjusting my necktie, at the same time making a running comment on the way some member of the party was dressed.''

It must not be supposed, however, that Homer's every waking moment was given over to Billy Sunday. The entrepreneur in him was just too strong for that.

In 1910 a music publishing house known as the Rode-heaver-Ackley Company was formed in Chicago; partner Bentley Ackley was Sunday's campaign pianist and confidential secretary. He was also a prolific songwriter. The new company published just one book, a song collection titled *Great Revival Hymns,* and then, in 1911, Homer became the sole owner. The Rodeheaver Company, destined for a long and prosperous life, was born, managed by his eldest brother, Yumbert.

It was also in 1910 that Rodeheaver began to record gospel songs for the likes of Victor, Columbia, and Edison. But it was not an entirely happy situation. As he travelled with the Sunday team he found that record dealers in the big cities simply were not getting enough copies of his records from the manufacturers to meet customer demands, a clear affront to the ambitious young man.

He would write: "Since none of the large Eastern [record] companies are trying or able to supply this demand, the idea has been steadily growing with me, why not counteract, in a way at least, the tremendous wave of popular songs and jazz music on the phonograph records, by giving the people something they really want in the way of sacred songs and a better grade of music?"

By 1920, he founded Rainbow Records. He had already, a year earlier, set the stage for getting deeply involved in the teaching of Christian song leaders by conducting the first "Song Directors Conference" in rural Winona Lake, Indiana, where Homer owned a summer cottage.

In modern terminology, Homer Rodeheaver was building a gospel music *conglomerate:* music publisher, recording company, song leaders training school—plus a print publishing arm to turn out songbooks and how-to texts for Sunday school, churches, choirs, et al., along with trade publications to promote it all. And all the while he was touring with Billy Sunday.

But in the closing months of 1918, he took time off from Sunday to go to France under the aegis of the Young Men's Christian Association to conduct song services for American soldiers. Again, in 1923 to 1924, he took a leave of absence from the Billy Sunday organization to go on a worldwide tour with his earlier evangelistic associate, the Reverend William Biederwolf, covering the Philippines, Korea, Japan, Australia, India, and Egypt.

Homer did return to the Sunday team after the world tour but the closeness of the Sunday-Rodeheaver pairing was not the same as it had been at its inception. By 1927, the association was virtually ended. First, there was a change in Billy that saw him show uncharacteristic irritability to others, Rodeheaver included, on the platform; secondly, Rodeheaver's own interests were taking more and more of his time, and that included his own evangelistic appearances.

While the book he was to write later would be titled *My Twenty Years with Billy Sunday*, it might more properly have been titled *My Seventeen Years* ... It would be foolish to deny that money didn't have something to do with the eventual breakup. Rodeheaver's outside interests were bringing in four times more than he was making with Sunday, and he was upset about his comparatively small income from the evangelistic campaigns. He believed he worked every bit as hard as Sunday and "when all ... things are compared," he told Billy in a letter, "I have been giving more than value received."

Sunday went into semiretirement in 1931 and died in 1935. Billy and Homer were still friends at the end, despite some differences. The friendship was based on mutual respect, one warrior to another in the never-ending battle for souls.

A new phase of Rodeheaver's life—one without the dominating figure of Billy Sunday—now began. In 1936, the Rodeheaver Company purchased its rival Hall-Mack Company of Philadelphia, to become the largest religious music publishing company in the country.

Also in 1936, Rodeheaver toured the mission fields of the Belgian Congo, hoping to find the origin of Negro spirituals. He had released Rainbow recordings of spirituals sung by the noted Fisk Jubilee Singers of Nashville, and the background of the spirituals fascinated him. When he returned he wrote a small book, *Singing Black: Twenty Thousand Miles with a Music Missionary,* expounding his theories and his conclusion.

In sum it was simplicity itself, no doubt too simplistic: "There is a theory that these [Negro spiritual] melodies originated in Africa but this I seriously question. Perhaps something of the rhythm came from there, but not the melody or harmony. As nearly as I can ascertain, no heathen country has melody or harmony. These two arts come to a people only after Jesus has been presented and accepted. 'Jesus Set the World to Singing!' Isn't that an incentive for us to try to get the people to sing, especially those in far away lands? Isn't it also an indication that peace, and melody, and harmony may be brought to the world if we can have more music 'of the people, for the people, and by the people'?"

Homer's personal-appearance schedule for the thirties and forties was backbreaking. He turned down few engagements; he was the subject of newspaper and magazine articles everywhere he went, most especially when he directed huge choirs, which he did frequently. In his very busy 1936, he was hired by a Chicago newspaper to lead the singing at the end of a summer music festival, directing eighty-five thousand people who were jammed into Soldier Field. He stood on a tower in the middle of the field, an imposing figure as he rehearsed and *controlled* a massive and ultimately melodious community sing.

Once, when he was with Billy Sunday, Rodeheaver put together a choir of some sixty-two thousand voices in the Atlantic City Auditorium. And in 1940 he topped everything else he had done before. Elwood, Indiana, was staging a homecoming for native son Wendell L. Willkie, the Republican presidential hopeful. A quarter of a million people gathered there to salute Willkie and Homer Rodeheaver actually led them in simultaneous song.

He was heard regularly on both the National and Columbia radio broadcasting networks and there was no performance venue he shunned.

In 1940 Rodeheaver began to invest in a ranch of some thirty-six thousand acres near Palatka, Florida. It was a livestock operation basically, but also encompassed a substantial timber business.

Growing out of all of that was something even more important to Homer. By 1950 he had used part of the land to establish a ranch for underprivileged boys. "Better to build boys than mend men," Rodeheaver said.

Any summary of the colorful life of Homer Alvan Rodeheaver must include his two-decade association with evangelist Billy Sunday. But there's more lasting value apparent in two other phases of Rodeheaver's days.

One was the evangelistic singing school at Winona Lake, Indiana, where thousands of future Christian song leaders were trained. The other, obviously, was the big music publishing house—The Rodeheaver Company.

Rodeheaver has only a few songs written by himself in the substantial catalog of The Rodeheaver Company. Perhaps the best of those is "You Must Open the Door," with lyrics by Ina Duley Ogdon, who was also the lyricist on the classic "Brighten the Corner Where You Are," which was practically the theme song of the Billy Sunday revival meetings:

> *Brighten the corner where you are!*
> *Brighten the corner where you are!*
> *Someone far from harbor you may guide*
> *across the bar,*
> *Brighten the corner where you are.*

(A fascinating gospel music statistic would emerge were it possible to complete a meaningful survey of the number of times Salvation Army street-corner bands have played that tune.)

Along with "Brighten the Corner," the Rodeheaver Company catalog became widely known for its gospel gems: "The Old Rugged Cross" (George Bennard), "Since Jesus Came Into My Heart" (Charles H. Gabriel and Rufus Henry McDaniel), "In the Garden" (C. Austin Miles), "Just As I Am" (William Bradbury and Charlotte Elliot), and "Sail On!" (Charles H. Gabriel), to mention only a few.

More than a decade after Homer's death—he died of a cerebral hemorrhage on December 18, 1955, at the age of seventy-five—the music publishing company was sold to Word, Inc., of Waco, Texas (July, 1969), and became known as Rodeheaver-Word Music. Then, in November of 1974, the American Broadcasting Company bought Word, it became a division of ABC, and the Rodeheaver name was lost in the corporate shuffle.

One imagines that the man himself would not be too distressed by the developments of his company. Its true assets, after all—the superb gospel music—are being cared for and preserved. And Homer Alvan Rodeheaver would understand the necessary corporate machinations perfectly.

No doubt he would smile his trademark smile, point to his colorful stationery, which carried a distinctive rainbow, and sing out his philosophy from the two lines of a gospel tune printed there:

> *Ev'ry cloud will wear a rainbow,*
> *If your heart keeps right.*

4

The Gospel Families

THE CHRISTIAN FAMILY HAS LONG BEEN A STAPLE OF gospel music's heritage: many families from many backgrounds. But five families, all with southern gospel roots, can be said to have cut the path and set the standards for American religious music in the twentieth century. Their names are still vital in gospel music today: the Vaughans and the LeFevres from Tennessee, the Stamps from Texas, the Speers from Alabama, and the Blackwoods from Mississippi.

All have had generally parallel careers and their stories often intertwine. All are recognized in the Gospel Music Hall of Fame for their exceptional contributions to Christian music.

So much began with the Vaughan name that it can be suggested that all of the major families of note spun off from it. James D. Vaughan, the motivator, was a product of the shaped note singing schools so prominent in the South in that period spanning the end of one century and the beginning of another. He understood that an opportunity existed beyond the singing schools:

a way to reach the masses of people, especially those desiring Christian music. In 1902, James, with brother Charles as a partner, founded the J. D. Vaughan Publishing Company in Lawrenceburg, Tennessee, for songbooks, textbooks, teaching aids, and a chatty little monthly, developed as a selling tool, called *The Vaughan Family Visitor*. The U.S. mail would be his ally.

It was immediately successful. By 1911, the Vaughan School of Music was opened, Christian students flooded in, and from among the best of them were formed quartets to be sent around the South to entertain and to promote the songs and books of the publishing company. James Vaughan also recognized the value of the new phenomenon of radio, building radio station WOAN, in Lawrenceburg—the first station in Tennessee. Thus, the Vaughan Quartet was the first sacred music group to perform on radio.

Included in that trend-setting quartet was James's son, Glen Kieffer Vaughan, and Glen's Uncle Charles. It would be Glen who would guide the various quartets carrying the family name over the years. They seemed to be everywhere, seeded through the South, influencing several generations of gospel music personalities yet to come.

It has been suggested that the Vaughan name is the rock on which much of today's gospel music was built—and promoted.

One who worked for the J. D. Vaughan company was a young man from Texas named V. O. (for Virgil Oliver) Stamps. The job with Vaughan was a launching pad for Stamps's ambitions. In 1924 he founded the V. O. Stamps Music Company and simultaneously opened the V. O. Stamps School of Music. Two years later, J. R. "Pap" Baxter, a superb teacher of harmony, joined the

Stamps company as a partner and the name was changed to Stamps-Baxter Music Company. Dallas was its base.

Taking a page from Vaughan's book, the Stamps music school immediately began to develop four-part harmony quartets to promote the company and sing its copyrighted songs. But V. O. did it bigger than Vaughan: at one time there were no less than one hundred Stamps Quartets placed on radio stations around the country. Such proliferation led to considerable confusion, so much so that Virgil had to call his own personal quartet, with which he sang bass, "The Old Original Quartet."

With his brother Frank and partner Baxter, V. O. built the world's largest music company dealing solely with gospel material. He had eclipsed the Vaughan company.

Once again, numerous substantial gospel music careers were started by association with Stamps quartets. It's still happening today, if in a less hectic atmosphere.

When the Gospel Music Hall of Fame was founded in 1971 the list was led by Tom "Dad" Speer. A year later his wife, Lena Brock Speer, was voted into the Hall of Fame. And in 1975, their eldest son, Brock Speer, was so honored. By that time Brock was in his fiftieth year of singing gospel music. He's still active in 1994.

Here again there was a Vaughan and Stamps connection. Tom Speer was a farmboy turned music teacher, working at one time or another with both the Vaughan and Stamps companies. So did his wife, Lena; her brother, Dwight Brock, was a Stamps singer and later would become the president of the company.

When Tom Speer formed the first Speer Quartet in 1921, he set the tone for the group with a simple philosophy: "Always sing what you feel and always feel what you sing." That has been the hallmark of the Speer family singers ever since.

In 1921 gospel quartets had only male members. Speer, however, now offered a quartet with two female singers—his wife of less than a year, Lena, and his sister Pearl. Brother-in-law Logan Claborn was the fourth member.

That was also an era when quartets offered a mixture of secular and religious music in their concerts, feeling it was necessary to draw audiences. Again Tom defied convention, decreeing that his quartet would sing *only* gospel music. His contemporaries told him he was wrong; Speer persisted and was successful. Eventually the contemporaries followed his lead and a whole new era was begun: that of all-gospel concerts.

Tom and Lena married in February of 1920; son Brock was born in December of the same year. Tom was fond of saying, "I met Lena, a singer's daughter originally, at a singing convention, married her in a singer's home, and raised a family of singers." That was true enough. Rosa Nell was born in 1922, Mary Tom in 1925, and Ben in 1930.

From the time the children were old enough to talk they were taught the rudiments of singing, including four-part harmony. Once the Claborns, Pearl and Logan, left the original quartet, the children became part of the group.

Brock recalled: "I guess I sang my first song with my parents in about 1925, when I was four or five years old. And about the same time me and Rosa Nell started singing a few songs on each program. At that time I sang alto, Rosa Nell sang soprano and, literally, Daddy sang bass and Momma sang tenor." Mary Tom and Ben also joined the family act at an early age.

Most of their performances in those early days were

at all-day singing and dinner-on-the-ground events. But many of the churches wouldn't accept them—a common enough reality with other early gospel groups as well. "They said our style of gospel was too jazzy [for churches] and was show music," Brock explained, "The kind of music you pat your foot to, and they didn't want anything that you could pat your foot to . . .

"When we first started out, we travelled by mule and wagon. I guess I'll never forget those mules—Kate and Beck. They took us a lot of places back then. I guess the farthest we could travel in a day was ten miles, but with Kate and Beck that took quite a while."

Tom Speer owned a farm then and he realized before long that he could make more money as a singer than as a farmer. The farm was sold, part of the money being used to buy a secondhand Model-T Ford. It was then that the Speer Family Singers became a full-time touring gospel act.

Eventually, they also turned to radio, appearing first on WSFA, Montgomery, Alabama, where they offered a Stamps-Baxter Music Company songbook, *Radio Selections No. 1*, for one dollar. Preachers who wrote in got a free copy. The mail poured in. The Speers would also pioneer in television in later years, both on the local station and syndication levels.

In 1946, "Dad" Speer, concerned with educational opportunities for his children, moved the family to Nashville. Brock, the eldest, believing he was being called as a preacher, enrolled in Trevecca Nazarene College and then went on to earn his Bachelor of Divinity degree at Vanderbilt University.

"I preached a little at revivals after that," Brock said, "but I never felt comfortable. I always felt the Lord was trying to tell me something else. I don't think my schooling was in vain, but I felt God's calling for me was to sing."

And sing they did, presenting many of the six hundred songs written by "Dad" Speer, all of them a reaffirmation of his unswerving faith. An excellent example is his "He Is Mine and I Am His":

Now that I know He is mine and I am His forever,
He is leading me along life's way;
He'll be holding my hand when I cross death's river,
He will take the sting of death away.

Tom died in 1966, at the age of 75; "Mom" Speer followed him in 1967—she was 67.

In the years since, the Speer Family Singers have had numerous personnel changes, going into a third generation of Speers. They became leaders in the Gospel Music Association. Ben built a substantial music publishing company. Of the more than seventy albums they produced, four won Grammy Awards; seven times they won the GMA's Dove Award as gospel music's best mixed group.

The 1994 Speer Family act consists of Brock and his wife Faye (a Kentucky preacher's daughter), brother Ben, and "adopted Speers" soprano Karen Apple and tenor Daryl Williams.

Over nearly three-quarters of a century the Speers have clearly earned the title of "First Family of Gospel Music."

Brock says: "We're having too much fun to retire."

In the same year (1921) that the Speer family singers began their career, so too did the LeFevre family of the tiny community of Smithville, Tennessee, in the Cumberland foothills some sixty miles due east of Nashville. It was a modest beginning for brothers Urias and Alphus LeFevre, for the first part of their journey along the road to ultimate gospel music fame was on foot. They walked to little churches in their immediate vicinity to perform their early gospel songs, sometimes accompanied by their sister Maude.

Both boys seemed blessed with natural music talent, but Alphus especially so. By the age of five he had taught himself to play a five-string banjo, later adding violin, piano and organ, guitar, and accordion. He had no money for formal lessons but learned some things by standing under an open window at the home of a local music teacher, eavesdropping on the lessons and learning most by the mistakes being made and the teacher's corrections. By age eight, Alphus was getting formal violin lessons from a teacher who had heard of the youngster's native talent and volunteered her services.

There was a time when Alphus thought of becoming a concert pianist but gave up that option for the gospel work.

The two young men played everywhere they could, earning nickles and dimes at first. They acquired a horse and buggy that enabled them to expand their territory, if only by a few miles. By careful saving, the LeFevres accumulated enough money to buy a used Ford truck of the "Chuck Wagon" model. Suddenly their range seemed unlimited.

However, the brothers had the same difficulties that were visited upon other touring acts—both gospel and country—in the early days of the Great Depression. Most roads across the nation were not built for gasoline-powered vehicles. Dirt "highways" turned to instant mud traps when it rained. Tires blew frequently because of the rocky ruts in most roads. So-called "service stations" were few and far between. Cars and trucks were not equipped with the niceties of heaters and air conditioners—thus passengers froze in the winter and boiled in the summer. But the internal combustion engine, with all its early maddening inconsistencies, *did* enable the gospel groups to travel great distances, spreading the joy of the Word of God as they conquered the miles.

Urias and Alphus, mindful of their need for higher education, both enrolled at Lee College in Cleveland, Tennessee. There, the family record has it, Urias met Eva Mae Whittington, daughter of a South Carolina pastor, who, in 1933, joined the brothers as alto vocalist, pianist, and emcee, launching the justly famous LeFevre Trio. Urias and Eva Mae married on September 9, 1934, and her contribution to the great success of the LeFevre musical family cannot be overstated.

(There is one delightful little tale that says Urias first laid eyes on Eva Mae when she was only eight years old—a pretty preacher's daughter playing piano in a rural Baptist church. It is said that Urias, then only sixteen himself, vowed to brother Alphus that he would marry the girl when she grew up. The meeting, then, at Lee College years later, was certainly fortuitous.)

From the union came five children: Pierce, Meurice, Monteia, Andrew, and Mylon, all of whom would play a role in the LeFevre family saga.

On the strength of the trio of Urias, Alphus, and Eva Mae, the act prospered as a thoroughly professional organization. Headquartering in Atlanta, the LeFevres built a large gospel music company to handle their activities in commercial radio shows for SunCrest Bottling and Martha White Flour (also the sponsors of the Flatt and Scruggs bluegrass band), television syndication with "Gospel Caravan" and "America Sings," and a publishing and production company called Sing Music Company, responsible for a line of songbooks, sheet music, and recordings—including their own, eschewing the major labels in Nashville.

They also brought in some consummate professionals

to become part of the family organization. Among them was Connor B. Hall, who had sung tenor with the LeFevres in the early forties and then went on to organize the immensely popular Homeland Harmony Quartet, which he brought to prominence by the judicious use of television and a vigorous promotional and merchandising program. Then, in the late fifties, he returned to the LeFevre fold, working his promotional magic as president of the family's Sing Music Company. Connor Hall was elected to the Gospel Music Hall of Fame.

So, too, was James Parks "Big Jim" Waites, a legendary bass singer in gospel music (maybe the best ever), who served a stint as a member of the LeFevre act. Waites was in great demand and would sing with the greatest gospel quartets of all time: Morros-Henson, Electrical Workers, Vaughan, Stamps, John Daniel, Homeland Harmony, The Rebels, and the LeFevres.

Then there was bass singer Rex Nelon, who had been part of Connor Hall's Homeland Harmony quartet and who joined the LeFevres in 1957. It was to be a long, long association.

As the LeFevre children joined the act it went more and more to variety, even though the gospel message was undiminished. Eldest son Pierce detailed what the performances offered: "You hear organ, piano, accordion, rhythm guitar, bass guitar, electric guitar, and trumpet. You hear solos, duets, trios, quartets, quintets, and sextets. When, in most quartets a man always sings the same part, every member of the LeFevre group sings at least two parts and plays two or more of the instruments."

Pierce wrote those words in his liner notes for a 1960 album *LeFevres in Hi-Fi* (Sing Music 3206), in which the youngest LeFevre, Mylon Rae, is introduced; a teenager described by his brother as "one of the most dynamic personalities I have ever seen in the stage.'' And so he was to be.

Eva Mae LeFevre, a woman who is universally popular, was elected to the Gospel Music Hall of Fame in 1977. Her husband, Urias, was posthumously honored in the Hall of Fame in 1986.

By that time much had changed with the LeFevres. The keeping alive of their traditional Southern gospel sounds had fallen to their longtime bass singer, Rex Nelon. The Rex Nelon singers have been presenting Eva Mae in special concert appearances in recent years.

And the youngest LeFevre, Mylon, has played a prominent—and, at times, troubled—role in gospel music's contemporary scene. When he was a high school senior and only seventeen, Mylon's composition, ''Without Him,'' was recorded by Elvis Presley for one of his gospel albums. Because Presley had cut it, so did others; a startling total of 126 recordings of ''Without Him'' were made, setting off a blizzard of royalty checks.

''I don't know if you can imagine a seventeen or eighteen-year-old getting thousands and thousands of dollars all at once in the mail,'' Mylon said. ''I mean, being able to go out and buy a Corvette and just pay cash. It's hard to comprehend.''

And it was hard to live the life of the rock 'n roll musicians he admired. He, too, got hooked on drugs. It wasn't until he was thirty-five that he turned his life around, quit drugs, and started a band he called ''Broken Heart''—a contemporary Christian sound that dominated the eighties.

In 1989, however, Mylon suffered a major heart attack. And as he began a long recovery, Mylon LeFevre reckoned that ''I needed God to save me, and He did. I'm younger than I was five years ago. God has ... given me a new version. 'Broken Heart' has accomplished the vision He'd given me for a season. We were Christian rockers and our purpose was to evangelize to young people. Now my purpose is to share the Word of God with anybody, any age, anytime, anywhere.''

The new Mylon (one commentator suggested it was *Brand New Start, Part Two*) recorded an album titled *Faith, Hope & Love* (Star Song, 1993), with such supportive friends as Steven Curtis Chapman, Ricky Skaggs, Carman, 4HIM, Michael W. Smith, and Michael English.

Critics noted the newfound maturity demonstrated in the album, as well as the return, in a song titled ''Faithful,'' to an acoustic format more reminiscent of the old LeFevre sound. A reviewer wrote: ''I hope you will bask in the same warmth I felt from this release from one of the true warriors of the kingdom.''

No mention can be made of ''true warriors'' in the gospel music field without inclusion of the name Blackwood, most especially that of James Blackwood, who was elected to the Gospel Music Hall of Fame in 1974. The Blackwood Brothers Quartet, beginning in 1934, was a leader in the gospel genre almost from the start.

Emmett and Carrie Blackwood were sharecroppers in rural Mississippi. They raised their four children—Roy, Lena, Doyle, and James—as devout Christians, moved to worship at brush arbor meetings, where singing was the release from day-to-day tribulations. The Blackwoods were poor. Very poor. When James wanted to hear the great Vaughan Quartet on radio he had to walk three miles to a neighbor's home because the Blackwoods had no radio.

Perhaps it's difficult to explain, but there was a real desire among the Blackwood boys to be gospel singers. Doyle and James managed to attend a singing school. Doyle also found a discarded Russian balalaika and taught himself to play it. By 1934, the first Blackwood Brothers Quartet was formed: Roy singing tenor, James the lead, Doyle was bass, and Roy's son, R. W., sang baritone. There was a nineteen-year disparity in the ages of Roy and James, and cousin R. W. seemed more of a brother to James.

The Blackwoods took the only path open to them as gospel singers, playing small churches and singing for free to get exposure on radio stations. They were heard on both WJDX, Jackson, Mississippi, and KWKH, Shreveport, Louisiana. One who heard them was the music publisher and founder of the Stamps Quartet, Virgil Oliver Stamps.

Stamps approached the Blackwoods with a deal. He would replace their beat-up used car with a brand new one and would be their booking agent for a percentage. Of course, they were also expected to sell Stamps-Baxter songbooks along the way. The Blackwoods agreed and prospered. As with all such quartets, there were often personnel changes.

They moved their headquarters to Memphis in 1950, began recording for the big RCA Victor label in 1951, and in 1954 the Blackwood Brothers Quartet won the Arthur Godfrey Talent Show on network television. The quartet then consisted of James and R. W. Blackwood, bass Bill Lyles, and tenor Bill Shaw.

In 1954, after their triumph on the Arthur Godfrey Show, they were to play the Peach Festival at Clanton, Alabama. R. W., the licensed pilot of the family airplane, was concerned about the shortness of the field at Clanton, and elected to try a practice takeoff before they loaded up for the return to Memphis. Bill Lyles went along with him on the practice run. They crashed; both were killed.

There was never any thought that the tragedy would mark the end of the Blackwood Brothers Quartet. R. W.'s younger brother, Cecil, immediately stepped into the act, and James sought out an experienced bass singer, J. D. Sumner, to replace Lyles. The changes would mark a new era for the Blackwoods.

Sumner, born in Lakeland, Florida, in 1924, had been influenced to be a singer in his earliest days when his mother took him to Pentecostal camp meetings each summer.

"One year the Homeland Harmony Quartet came to our camp meeting," Sumner recalled, "and another year Frank Stamps himself came and sang 'Stand By Me.' I was told by my mother that one day, when I was four years old, someone asked me what I wanted to be when I grew up, and I said I was going to be a bass singer in a gospel quartet." He laughed heartily.

In 1945, after a short stint in the Army, J. D. did reach that goal, singing first with the Sunny South Quartet in Tampa. Later he went with the busy Sunshine Boys who made "B"-movie westerns with Charles Starrett and Smiley Burnette, were featured on the "barn dance" radio program on WSB, Atlanta, and became the top act on the Wheeling, West Virginia, Jamboree on WWVA Radio. The Sunshine Boys also sang background on country star Red Foley's million-seller record of "Peace In the Valley."

Sumner didn't hesitate, however, when the call came from James Blackwood in 1954. He and James soon became partners in innovation; the Blackwood Brothers became the first touring act to use a customized bus for their travel. "The Blackwoods came to Nashville in our bus," J. D. remembers, "and Hawkshaw Hawkins, being a friend of mine from the Wheeling Jamboree days, came over and seen our bus. Hawkshaw then bought him an Airporter, a little flexible bus, and customized it and he was the first one in country music to use a bus."

In 1957, Blackwood and Sumner began the annual National Quartet Convention. "That was a dream of mine that came from the old camp meeting days," J. D. said. "What I really had in mind was a Gospel Quartet Camp Meeting, where everybody'd get together once a year.

"We put it in Memphis in '57 and it was very much of a success for three days. And we had the idea then that we ought to move it around from town to town. So we went to Birmingham in '58 and that wasn't near as good as Memphis. We went to Atlanta the next year and that was even worse. So we came back to Memphis and kept it there until 1965, when I moved to Nashville and moved the Gospel Quartet Convention there as well."

One of the most important moves made by James Blackwell and J. D. Sumner was in 1962 when they purchased the Stamps Quartet Music Company, also acquiring the rights to the landmark Stamps Quartet. Personnel changes were made, going to younger singers, and in 1965 Sumner left the Blackwood Brothers Quartet to become the manager of what would thereafter be called "J. D. Sumner and the Stamps Quartet."

"James and I still owned the Blackwood Brothers and the Stamps Quartet and two music companies— Stamps Quartet Music and Gospel Quartet Music," J. D. explained. "But in 1970 we decided to split it up. James kept the Blackwoods and Stamps Music, and I kept the Stamps Quartet and Gospel Quartet Music, because all of my songs, more than five hundred, had the copyrights in Gospel Quartet Music."

Anyone who knows J. D. Sumner recognizes that he is a man who speaks his mind. And while he understands that the diversity of today's gospel is important to the well-being of the genre, he questions what he regards as "too much preaching" by many of the contemporary gospel artists.

"We're Christians, but we're also professional singers," he says, "and when you charge admission for people to get in to hear you then it should be *entertainment.* For Christian people.

"Back in the old quartet days, when I first started, we used to go into our concerts and sing fifteen minutes of gospel music, then fifteen minutes of western music, cowboy music, then we'd have fifteen minutes of comedy, and fifteen minutes of 'pop'—something like 'Old Buttermilk Sky' and 'Rag Mop' (we sang that for years), then we'd close our concert with fifteen minutes more of gospel. It was like saying, 'Wow, you can have fun and still be a Christian.' "

Sumner pointed to the days when the Blackwood Brothers performed with Elvis Presley, recalling: "One time I took [evangelist] Rex Humbard and his wife, Maude Amy, to meet Elvis. And we talked for two hours. Elvis loved gospel music—I think it was his first love—and he asked Humbard, 'Do you think I should go and sing nothing but gospel music?' And Rex said, 'By no means. But by having gospel music entwined in your show, by singing "How Great Thou Art" and other gospel songs, you are tilling the soil so that people like us can plant the seed.'

"Now, I agree with that. I don't believe in a quartet, or any other gospel singers, wearing their ministry out on their sleeves, in getting up and preaching and over-testifying. I believe in entertaining the people with good singing, so they can forget their troubles, and then let the song itself be the ministry.

"After all, that's why it's gospel music!"

5

Thomas A. Dorsey

THE LIFE STORY OF GEORGIA TOM DORSEY, A LEGEND
in both the blues and gospel music fields, may best be
described as enigmatic, a puzzling array of contradictions. On one hand, the preacher's son Tom Dorsey had
tap roots in the Protestant Christian faith, so deep they
could not be pulled up. On the other hand, the musician
Georgia Tom—pianist, composer, and arranger of semi-
nal blues—did what he had to do to survive in difficult times.

The opposing pulls of the contradictions would take
their toll on the health of the slightly built black man
who had never been physically strong. But, having survived, the tap roots prevailed. He had been a topnotch
blues man; he would be a better gospel man. Against
that simple summation, then, the story of Thomas Andrew Dorsey can best be told.

Born on July 1, 1899, in the tiny village of Villa
Rica, Georgia—hard by the tracks of the Southern Railroad—about thirty miles from Atlanta, he was the first
child of the Reverend Thomas Madison Dorsey and

Etta (nee Plant) Dorsey. They were a couple with social status in Villa Rica: the elder Thomas was a college-trained preacher and part-time school teacher and Mrs. Dorsey was a woman of property—a rarity in those post-emancipation days in the South. Etta had been married to a railroader, who had been killed on the job; insurance money enabled her to buy some land in Villa Rica.

But those seeming advantages did not make them solvent. Reverend Dorsey was not always "employed." He was an "itinerant revival-running preacher," as young Tom would describe him years later, who was often away for periods of two to three weeks at a time conducting his revival meetings. The son would look forward to his homecomings because there would always be a special treat—a cake or pie.

Tom admired his father; he would "play preacher" under the high porch of his home, imitating the mannerisms of the elder Dorsey. "I liked to [travel] with him because they fed well at these revivals," Tom recalled. "In the summertime everybody'd bring a basket on Sunday, and fill it full of food and spread tablecloths on the ground, and everybody came and ate. For nothin'."

Black revival meetings in the first decade of the twentieth century didn't pay preachers very well; "good will" offerings were meager. The Dorseys tried share-crop farming and failed. By 1910, the family moved to Atlanta, hoping to find paying jobs. Young Tom walked the family milk cow, "Lily," all the way from Villa Rica to Atlanta. Things went from bad to worse; the cow would have to be sold, it was decided, to get money to eat. Tom walked "Lily" to the slaughter-house, a traumatic experience for the youngster.

But there were some moments of joy in his childhood. One he recalled vividly was attendance at a Billy Sunday revival meeting on the circus grounds in Atlanta. Tom was there on what was designated as "Colored Night." The big tent was packed and Dorsey recalled that "when Sunday got hot, he'd take off his coat and loosen his collar and everybody would holler 'Amen' and 'Hallelujah.' It must have been just a gesture but the people went wild."

Dorsey was particularly taken with the work of Sunday's musician and song leader, Homer Rodeheaver. He could not have imagined then that in the years ahead he would become a friend of Rodeheaver and do business with his publishing company in Chicago.

The strained fiscal circumstances of the Dorsey family would find the boy going to the 81 Theater (81 Decatur Street in Atlanta), where he got a job as the "butch boy," selling pop (soft drinks) and popcorn during intermissions. The 81 Theater and the 91 Theater, a block away, were two of at least five film and vaudeville houses for the black population of the city. And all of those establishments employed pianists.

In a wide-ranging interview with Jim and Amy O'Neal, Dorsey spoke of his earliest musical training: "I got my blues experience when I was a young boy about ten at the old 81 Theater. . . . And I remember Ed Butler was the pianist there that played for the shows. . . . Another fellow was a good friend of ours called Long Boy, he played a little bit. But Eddie Heywood soon came, he came about 1912 or 1913 or maybe 1911. Now not the fellow who wrote 'Canadian Sunset,' but his father. And that's where I began to get the show experience . . . and I learned a lot of music there.

"For see, those fellows who played there read music. I learned to read—they taught me, and I got very interested in it."

Dorsey was determined to join the ranks of the pianists he admired. He would walk four miles a day, four days a week, to take fifty-cent lessons from a piano teacher named Mrs. Graves, who had a studio very near Morehouse College, where his father had trained as a preacher.

He told author Michael W. Harris that with Mrs. Graves he "took, I think, maybe the first grade of music. Well, heck, I felt . . . that's all I need to know about music. I'm quick."

In a very short time the teenager joined the ranks of such Saturday night stomp piano players as Long Boy, Lark Lee, Soap Stick, Nome Burkes, Harvey Squiggs, and Charlie Spann, earning the sobriquet of "Barrelhouse Tom." Dorsey was soon recognized as something special by those who promoted the "stomps" (dances); when other pianists were earning fifty cents a night, Tom could command a dollar and a half.

He played where he could: at the "stomps," in bordellos, and at rowdy, after-hours house parties that proliferated during prohibition. It was the house parties, where varied forms of dancing and intimate association prevailed, that led him to develop a style of playing he called "slow drag."

Dorsey explained to author Michael Harris that some of his contemporaries working house parties "play loud and folk got loud and [somebody would] call the law. But I played soft and easy, you could drag it out and hug the woman at the same time. Let the lights down low and they'd have to give attention to hear the piano."

But the ambitious Tom Dorsey was a realist; he knew he wasn't really getting anywhere. He certainly wasn't making much money in Atlanta.

"Seemed the old town did not have much charm for me anymore," he wrote in his self-published memoirs. "I had a yearning to move up higher. . . . I wanted bigger and better things and I wanted to go where the lights were brighter and you didn't have to run to get the last streetcar at midnight.''

He set his eyes on Chicago. "They said it was a place of freedom," he could recall. "I was looking for that."

However, Georgia Tom would approach burgeoning Chicago with a certain hesitancy. He went there for the first time in July of 1916, working odd jobs and playing piano at house parties similar to those in Atlanta. When winter came, Chicago was too cold for him and he returned to Atlanta. He would repeat that back-and-forth cycle for the next two years, finally settling in Chicago in the latter part of 1919. He was only one of the thousands of southern blacks who were pouring into Chicago. Between 1910 and 1920, the black population of the city had increased by some 150 percent.

In truth, his early piano-playing jobs in Chicago offered venues that were very much like those he had been working in Atlanta: rent parties in private houses, wine rooms (for women drinkers), and a unique Chicago prostitution institution called "buffet flats," run by "landladies." Indeed, those landladies particularly admired his soft, easy style of playing because, as in Atlanta, it was less likely to attract the attention of the police. He was called the "whispering piano player" and was frequently employed at the "buffet flats."

He understood his predicament. He had not really put himself in the position to "move up higher"; he was not approaching "bigger and better things." He wisely entered the Chicago School of Composition and Arranging, and by October 9, 1920, he had copyrighted his first blues composition: "If You Don't Believe I'm Leaving, You Can Count the Days I'm Gone."

Just when it seemed he was taking a step forward, his schedule of playing parties and buffet flats far into the night and working at other jobs during the day caught up with him. He became ill, suffering what was called a nervous breakdown. His weight had fallen off dramatically; he was just skin and bones. Finally his mother travelled to Chicago to take him home to Atlanta, where she could care for him.

He was just twenty-one years old and was at a crossroads in his life.

By the late summer of 1921, he was sufficiently recovered from his illness to return to Chicago and try to pick up the pieces of his musical career. He was apparently living with an uncle, Joshua Dorsey, a Chicago druggist. The uncle urged him to attend the final session of the all-black National Baptist Convention being held at the Eighth Regiment Armory. The date was Sunday, September 11, 1921.

The convention session was not what Tom had expected. He watched as young ladies in starched white outfits, and men in tuxedos, Prince Albert coats, cutaways and silk hats, paraded about. The *Chicago Defender,* the city's prominent black newspaper, reported that "iron-throated vendors of the blattering of some puny scribbler in Massachusetts or Louisiana tramped the aisles of the great hall filching the pockets of the unsuspecting of their money for a few dry and empty pages. Everything was sold in the floor from hair tonic to a man's soul."

But there was also a worship service in the armory during which a charismatic evangelist, "Professor" W. M. Nix, performed a gospel song titled "I Do, Don't You?"—ironically written by a white man, E. O. Excell, the flamboyant song leader for Georgia evangelist Sam Jones:

> *I know a great Savior,*
> *I do; don't you?*

I live by His favor,
I do; don't you?
For grace I implore Him,
I worship before Him,
I love and adore Him,
I do; don't you?

Nix's performance thrilled Tom Dorsey, filled as it was by a bluesy type of improvisation and genuine emotion. "The whole text was good news," Dorsey said. And he would write later that his "heart was inspired to become a great singer and worker in the Kingdom of the Lord."

Tom meant it—at the time. He joined the New Hope Baptist Church and began to write sacred songs, including "If I Don't Get There," which was to be his first copyrighted gospel song:

Dear friends and kindreds have gone from this world,
To dwell in that city so fair,
Hard trials and troubles no longer they share,
They'll be disappointed if I don't get there.

Years later, Dorsey would tell an interviewer: "I was converted to this gospel song business in 1921." However, that specific conversion didn't last too long. Reality set in; being a church musical director and/or writing gospel songs didn't pay well at all. Within just a few months he left the New Hope Baptist position to join the "Whispering Syncopators" orchestra when conductor Will Walker offered him a steady job at forty dollars a week.

It was a dance band that would also nurture the early talents of future jazz greats Les Hite and Lionel Hampton. There was a successful twelve-week tour of the midwest area, working theaters and nightclubs. But when a West Coast opportunity arose, under the aegis of white piano player Ben Harney, Dorsey wasn't invited to go along. The band didn't need *two* piano players.

There is nothing to indicate that Tom was disturbed by the failure to go to the West Coast. Opportunities as a composer, if not a performer, were rife in Chicago as the blues record market opened up. There was a growing demand for his blues compositions. Monette Moore recorded his "I Just Want A Daddy I Can Call My Own" and his "Muddy Water Blues." King Oliver's storied Creole Jazz Band recorded Dorsey's "Riverside Blues" on the Paramount label, for which Tom had become a sometime agent. It was Paramount that would offer Dorsey his next important opportunity.

The record label had just signed veteran black entertainer Gertrude "Ma" Rainey, billed as the "Mother of the Blues," and wanted to tour her with a package show to promote Paramount Records. To do that she needed a full-scale band and Tom Dorsey was called upon to put it together.

He would be the pianist/arranger, of course, and he hired Fuller Henderson on cornet, whose wife, Lil, would tour with them; Albert Wynn on trombone, Gabriel Washington on drums, and George Pollock (some believe it may have been *Eddie* Pollock) on saxophone. They were dubbed the "Wild Cats Jazz Band."

In April of 1924, the "Ma" Rainey tour was kicked off in Southside Chicago's prestigious Grand Theater. It was a triumph for Rainey, Dorsey, and Paramount Records. They took off across the country, booked by the giant Theater Owners' Booking Association.

In his self-published memoirs, Tom offered a lavish description of a Rainey performance:

"The room is filled with a haze of smoke, she walks into the spotlight, face decorated with Stein's Reddish

Make-up Powder. She's not a young symmetrical stream-lined type ... she stands out high in front with a glorious bust, squeezed tightly in the middle. Her torso, extended in the distance behind, goes on about its business from there on down. She opens her mouth and starts singing:

'It's storming on the ocean, it's storming on the sea,
My man left me this morning, and it's storming down
* on me.'*

"When she started singing, the gold in her teeth would sparkle. She was in the spotlight. She possessed her listeners; they swayed, they rocked, they moaned and groaned, as they felt the blues with her. A woman swooned who had lost her man. Men groaned who had given their week's pay to some woman who promised to be nice, but slipped away and couldn't be found at the appointed time. By this time she was just about at the end of her song. She was 'in her sins' as she bellowed out. The bass drum rolled like thunder and the stage lights flickered like forked lightning:

'I see the lighting flashing, I see the waves a-dashing
I got to spread the news; I feel this boat a-crashing
I got to spread the news; my man is gone and left me
Now I got the stormy sea blues.'

"As the song ends, she feels an understanding with her audience. Their applause is a rich reward. She is in her glory ..."

It's not surprising that Tom Dorsey would include "Stormy Sea Blues" in his story. He wrote it for Rainey; it was a major hit for both of them.

Tom married Nettie Harper, a Georgia-girl immigrant to Chicago, in August of 1925 and "Ma" Rainey hired the new Mrs. Dorsey as her wardrobe mistress. It was a viable job, for Rainey had what was known as a "flash" act. Perhaps to offset her homeliness, she wore colorful gaudy costumes, with feather boas and plumes, set off with a lot of jewelry: a necklace of five-, ten-, and twenty-dollar gold pieces, genuine diamonds, long earrings, and sparkling tiaras. Her love of jewelry nearly undid her.

The act was playing in Cleveland when detectives from Nashville, Tennessee, came on stage and arrested her. The story was that she had bought some "hot" jewelry—stolen property—in Nashville. The singer was away from her show for a week before returning to the tour. Dorsey was not told the specifics of what happened to her during that week. "Ma never did seem the same after that," Tom recalled. "I don't know why. She just didn't have the spirit that she used to."

Then, early in 1926, Dorsey became ill again, first noticing a slight "unsteadiness" while the Wild Cats Jazz Band was playing a club date on the outskirts of Chicago. The condition worsened, eventually preventing him from doing any work. Doctors were consulted, he spent two weeks in Cook County Hospital— no one could find anything wrong with him. But when he could not work, total despair set in. He thought of throwing himself into Lake Michigan.

Nettie Dorsey took a job in a laundry to support them. Tom's personal hell went on for eighteen months. Then his sister-in-law intervened, taking him to church and getting him to talk to the minister, Bishop H. H. Haley. "Brother Dorsey," the bishop said, "there is no reason for you to be looking so poorly and feeling so badly. The Lord has too much work for you to do to let you die."

There was then an incident in which the preacher pulled a "live serpent" out of his throat. Dorsey wrote that his ailment, whatever it was, then passed, and he pledged: "Lord, I am ready to do your work."

As his strength returned he started to write gospel songs again, including "Someday Somewhere":

> *Someday somewhere in a city so fair,*
> *Far away from these burdens and cares*
> *There'll be peace, there'll be joy*
> *There'll be riches I'll share*
> *When I reach that city over there.*

But nobody really wanted it, no publisher, no church choir, no record company. He attempted, then, to go to church services, offer himself as a singer to the pastor, and that way introduce "Someday Somewhere." One minister agreed to help him. And on Sunday morning he sat in a front pew waiting for his introduction. It never came. It was a humiliating experience. A job as an arranger for the Brunswick Recording Company was what enabled him to make a fiscal comeback and get his wife out of the laundry.

So, too, did a new association with a young guitarist and singer widely known as Tampa Red (Hudson Whittaker), who had come to Dorsey with a raunchy lyric titled "It's Tight Like That." Tom composed music for it. Vocalian Records immediately released it and it was a major hit. Dorsey's first royalty check was for $2,400.19—a substantial sum in his life at that juncture. His immediate money problems were ended. Tom and Tampa Red went on tour to take advantage of the popularity of the song and prospered further.

Some have suggested that blues music had "tempted" Dorsey and that he was ashamed of his association with the blues. Not so. "There was nothing wrong with the blues," he said in the 1975 *Living Blues* interview. "It was good music. . . . When I was singing blues I sang 'em with spirit. Now I've got gospel songs, I sing 'em with spirit, see? I don't care what you're singing ... there is something that comes, a vibration that comes from somewhere that makes you do extraordinary.... I can't name it. Some folk call it spirit. Some folk call it God. Some folk call it something else.... I don't know—all I know is about myself. Whatever it is, I like it.''

Thomas Andrew Dorsey, with all of his ups and downs, with all of his obvious enthusiasm for secular music, was never really far from his religious roots. And when he found a way to employ the syncopation of his blues songs in his gospel writing, and in gospel performance, he had finally achieved a new and bolder upturn in his life.

As the thirties began, Dorsey had positioned himself to make a complete switch to gospel music. His secular successes had given him the fiscal independence he had needed. And what was happening in Chicago's black churches was the emergence of what could only be called "gospel blues," in no small measure attributable to the presence of Georgia Tom.

It wasn't too long before Dorsey became associated with the big Ebenezer Baptist Church where a nontraditional gospel chorus was started in 1931 under the aegis of a "ball of fire" urban evangelist named Theodore Frye who benefitted from Tom's coaching in stage technique, adding an exaggerated strut to his performance. Dorsey was hired as Ebenezer's choral director, a position he would hold for forty years.

He also travelled widely, attending church conventions to promote his music and his newfound prominence as a choral director. Such a selling opportunity arose in 1932 when Dorsey went to a big revival meeting in St. Louis with a handy "batch of songs." He had left Chicago reluctantly because his wife was well advanced in a pregnancy; she insisted he go. The first night in St. Louis was a song-seller's delight. But on the second night, Tom received a telephone call from Chicago telling him that Hettie had died in childbirth. He rushed home to learn that the baby—a boy—had died as well.

He was heartbroken and in the depth of his despair he began to write a song. He said later that he didn't write the words, they just came to him. He played it for his friend, Reverend Frye, singing "Blessed Lord, take my hand . . ." Frye strongly recommended that he change the first phrase to "*Precious* Lord, take my hand . . ." After resisting at first, Tom accepted his advice. "Precious Lord, Take My Hand," reflecting his personal grief, would become Dorsey's first gospel megahit, recorded by virtually every gospel singer, black and white, and translated into thirty-two languages.

It was in 1932, also, that a young Georgia-born woman, Sallie Martin, joined Tom's Ebenezer Baptist gospel chorus. There were better singers, perhaps, but Sallie had some entrepreneurial skills as well. They became partners in publishing and in touring the nation to set up gospel choirs that would use their music. The duo also founded the Gospel Singers Convention, an annual convocation of black gospel singers around the country, of which Dorsey was the long-time president.

They also sponsored up-and-coming talent, including the superb Roberta Martin. The noted musicologist Anthony Heilbut wrote that "Dorsey and Sallie and Roberta Martin were constructing the 'gospel highway,' a circuit punctuated by churches and auditoriums where gospel groups were welcome."

Eventually, Tom and Sallie had a parting of the ways in their association but she had played a major role in his life. It's interesting to note that Sallie, in her own role as a publisher, was responsible for bringing to light the classic "Just A Closer Walk With Thee."

But by the end of the thirties, Tom Dorsey was clearly at the top of his game. Two leading white publishers of gospel music—Stamps-Baxter and R. E. Winsett—were releasing anthologies of Dorsey tunes. Homer Rodeheaver also published a pair of Dorsey songs that were indistinguishable from pop ballads: "It's My Desire" and "When I've Done the Best I Can." In the late forties band leader Guy Lombardo recorded a pop version of "My Desire." Then, too, Tom gave a big boost to the career of Mahalia Jackson, touring with her from 1939 to 1944.

But no one could have predicted what was going to happen when, in 1939, Dorsey adapted an old spiritual, "We Shall Walk Through the Valley in Peace," into what musicologist Tony Heilbut has described as "a plaintive semi-hillbilly hymn."

Enter Julian (Red) Foley, a charismatic Grand Ole Opry star and a substantial presence on recordings, network radio, and early television. Foley knew the things his country audiences liked and bought; his recording sessions always included a gospel song—in 1950 he recorded "Steal Away," with the Jordaines quartet, and the popular "Just A Closer Walk With Thee."

In 1951, his recording of Dorsey's "Peace in the Valley" became the first gospel record ever to sell a million copies. Eventually, "Steal Away" and "Just A Closer Walk With Thee" would also reach million-seller status. Foley would be the number-one sacred song performer on records for five consecutive years.

Red's routine was to close every concert appearance with "Peace in the Valley." On September 18, 1968, he was appearing in Fort Wayne, Indiana. But the show didn't go well that night. Foley told the large audience that he felt poorly and that he hoped the fans wouldn't mind if he closed a bit early. Then he sang:

> *I am tired and so weary,*
> *But I must go along*
> *'Til the Lord comes and calls me away . . .*
> *There'll be no sorrow, no sadness,*
> *No trouble I see,*
> *There'll be peace in the valley for me.*

Fittingly somehow, it was to be the last song he ever sang. He went back to his motel and died in his sleep during the early morning hours. He was only fifty-eight.

Just a year earlier, Foley had been inducted into the Country Music Hall of Fame; he said it was one of the proudest moments of his life. In October of 1968, when time came for another Hall of Fame induction, Foley's son-in-law, Pat Boone, appeared on the Country Music Association's awards telecast and movingly sang that same song, "Peace in the Valley," in tribute to one of the most versatile performers in any field. It could also have been regarded as a tribute to another versatile music man, Georgia Tom Dorsey.

(It should not be forgotten that a young man from Memphis by the name of Elvis Presley also had a million-seller record of "Peace in the Valley.")

Dorsey's life was not without its tributes. In 1979, he was inducted into the Hall of Fame of the Nashville Songwriters Association International. In the spring of 1982 he was named to the Gospel Music Association's Hall of Fame. In September of that same year he was given a special Broadcast Music Incorporated (BMI) citation in ceremonies at the New York Songwriters Hall of Fame, and in October of 1982 he was inducted into the Georgia Hall of Fame.

Although Tom was a naturally shy individual, he didn't turn away from those honors. He was proud, as well, of what he had accomplished, telling an interviewer: "People respect me." But he could not have been prepared for what happened during the observance of Gospel Music Week in 1981.

Those who were there will never forget it.

A highlight of Gospel Music Week was an April luncheon in the Stage Door Lounge restaurant at Nashville's plush Opryland Hotel. BMI's Joe Moscheo, the master of ceremonies of the event, had just introduced Tom Dorsey to a standing ovation.

As the elderly black man who had become both a blues and gospel legend rose slowly from his seat, Moscheo began to sing:

> *"Precious Lord, take my hand . . ."*

Instantly, the entire audience joined in:

> *"Lead me on, let me stand,*
> *I am tired, I am weak, I am worn . . ."*

"It was a moving moment," former Gospel Music Association executive director Don Butler recalls. "A lot of the people there had never met the man, had never even seen him before. Mr. Dorsey was quite feeble at the time, but the years seemed to fade away as the old man conducted the singing, while singing along."

> *"Through the storm, through the night*
> *Lead me on to the light . . ."*

Frances Preston, who just that week had been elected president of the Gospel Music Association (she is today the president of BMI), remembers: "The place was packed with all manner of gospel music singers and the rendition of Mr. Dorsey's song was very emotional. More than a few tears were shed."

> *"Take my hand, precious Lord,*
> *Lead me home."*

That song was sung again by the gospel music community when Dorsey died on January 23, 1993, in Chicago in his ninety-third year.

6

Mahalia Jackson

IT WAS WEDNESDAY, AUGUST 28, 1963, A SUNNY,
blue-skies day, somewhat breezy, and not the hot and
sticky summer day that might have been expected for
Washington, D.C. It was to be a historic day, covered
in depth by the television networks—the day of a civil
rights demonstration known formally as the March On
Washington for Jobs and Freedom.

Frank McGee of NBC News would report: "They
moved today two hundred thousand strong down a
broad and tree-shaded avenue in Washington, softly
singing and chanting the hymns born of their movement
and those that have gone before. There were no ranks,
but they were orderly. They moved with dignity, but
there was no sternness. Their placards demanded the
uprooting of every vestige of discrimination and said it
must be done *now,* but they showed no anger."

It was a day built on a foundation of soul-stirring
music. Joan Baez sang the civil rights anthem, "We
Shall Overcome." The great contralto Marian Anderson
offered "He's Got the Whole World in His Hands."

But it was Mahalia Jackson, of New Orleans and Chicago, who was asked by the Reverend Dr. Martin Luther King, Jr., to sing just before he was to speak, requesting his favorite spiritual, "I Been 'Buked and I Been Scorned."

The throng gathered at the Lincoln Memorial was mesmerized. Mahalia began it softly and gently in the traditional manner. But then something happened. "As I sang the words," she recalled, "I heard a great murmur come up from the multitude below, and I sensed I had reached out and touched a chord. I was moved to shout with joy, and I did! I lifted the rhythm to a gospel beat. The great crowd began singing and clapping, and joy overflowed."

There were cries of "More, more!" when she finished, and the listeners and marchers would not be denied. Mahalia moved into a gospel classic written by the outstanding black songwriter, the Rev. W. Herbert Brewster—"How I Got Over."

> *All night long, God sent his angels,*
> *watching over me,*
> *And early this morning, God told his angels,*
> *God said, touch her in my name,*
> *And I rose this morning . . .*

Her marvelous voice had set the stage for Reverend King and his stirring address:

"I have a dream that one day on the red hills of Georgia, the sons of former slaves and the sons of former slave-owners will be able to sit together at the table of brotherhood.

"I have a dream that one day even the State of Mississippi, a state sweltering in the heat of injustice, sweltering in the heat of oppression, will be transformed into an oasis of freedom and justice.

"I have a dream that my four little children will one day live in a nation where they will not be judged by the color of their skin, but by the content of their character . . .

"I have a dream that . . . from every state and every city, we will be able to speed up the day when all God's children, black men and white men, Jews and Gentiles, Protestants and Catholics, will be able to join hands and sing the words of that old Negro spiritual:

> *Free at last! Free at last!*
> *Thank God Almighty,*
> *We are free at last!*"

Clearly, Wednesday, August 28, 1963, would be regarded as Martin Luther King's day. But it would also be Mahalia Jackson's day. One newspaper columnist commented: "Of all of the entertainers, Mahalia Jackson plainly stirred things up the most. Marian Anderson was the most dignified, but Mahalia had them rockin' . . ."

Author Anthony Heilbut, writing in his book *The Gospel Sound,* called her "the vocal, physical, spiritual, symbol of gospel music. Her huge (260 pounds), noble proportions, her face contorted into something like the Mad Duchess, her soft speaking voice and huge, rich contralto, all made her gospel's superstar."

And for both black and white audiences.

Mahalia Jackson was born in New Orleans on October 26, 1911, the third of six children. Her father worked as a stevedore on the Mississippi River docks and as a sometimes barber. On Sundays, though, he was the preacher at a small black Baptist church. By the age of five she was singing in the choir of that church. The father was a strict disciplinarian. Although he had several sisters in vaudeville, and although New

Orleans was a hotbed of jazz, only sacred music could be heard in the Jackson household.

But two cousins, with whom she went to live after her mother died, introduced her to the blues recordings of Bessie Smith, Ida Cox, and Gertrude "Ma" Rainey. Some music critics insisted that Mahalia's vocal styling was influenced by those early blues singers; she always vehemently denied it.

Gospel singing is what she wanted to do, what she *insisted* on doing—because gospel songs were joyful, full of hope. "Anybody singing the blues," she would explain, "is in a deep pit yelling for help."

In the eighth grade she left school to work as a laundress and a maid. In the late twenties, at the age of only sixteen, she went to Chicago, intent on studying beauty culture or becoming a nurse. Instead, she was a hotel maid and a date-packer in a factory. But she was not easily discouraged. During the Great Depression days she toured with Robert Johnson and a group known as The Johnson Gospel Singers, a highly professional group started by the son of the pastor of Greater Salem Baptist. They would earn as much as eight dollars a night—on some nights.

The young singer from New Orleans also came under the considerable influence of Thomas A. Dorsey (*see* Chapter 5), a leading gospel musician, composer, and singers' coach in those days. When he first heard her sing he was more than a little impressed.

A later close friend of Mahalia, television producer and author Jules Schwerin, says Dorsey "soon realized that she was a natural-born singer who needed no outside direction, nor did she have the disposition to tolerate anyone's advice. He settled for introducing her and his songs to Chicago and out-of-town churches, where they were always ready to embrace a new gospel voice. The fees were small, but Mahalia didn't care as long as the publicity was substantial. Cannily, she figured that the fees would grow along with her reputation. By the time Mahalia became a star, Dorsey had dedicated a number of gospel songs to her and they became her trademark.''

Mahalia's stardom, however, was still a long way off. Her earlier ambition to become a beautician was not forgotten. She scraped together enough money to go to a beauty school and even to open a small beauty shop in Chicago. But the music in her was not to be denied.

In 1937, she made her first recording for Decca Records: ''God Gonna Separate the Wheat from the Tares,'' an adaptation from the New Orleans wakes of Mahalia's childhood:

> *If you never hear me sing no more,*
> *Aw, meet me on the other shore,*
> *God's gonna separate the wheat from the tares,*
> *Didn't He say.*

The record (with a Baptist hymn, ''Keep Me Every Day,'' on the ''B'' side) sold rather well in the South, yet the lightning of fame didn't strike her. She went on singing everywhere she could and it wasn't until the mid-forties that Apollo Records picked her up. And she had a top seller with ''Move On Up A Little Higher,'' written by the Memphis songwriting pastor W. Herbert Brewster.

Mahalia put her own distinctive touches on the song, improvising lyrics and cadences as she sang.

> *Put on my robe in glory and tell my story . . .*
> *How I come over hills and mountains . . .*
> *I'm goin' to drink from the crystal fountains . . .*
> *And move on up a little higher!*

Fanny Crosby as she was in 1872.

(Author's collection)

Ira D. Sankey at his organ in London.
(Author's collection)

Homer Rodeheaver (left) and Billy Sunday (right).
(Author's collection)

The Singing Speer Family in the early 1920's. (Left to right) Lena Speer, Tom Speer, Pearl Claborn, Logan Claborn. *(Author's collection)*

Mahalia Jackson at her finest.
(Author's collection)

The LeFevre Trio. (Left to right) Alphus LeFevre, Urias
LeFevre, Eva Mae LeFevre.   *(Author's collection)*

Thomas A. Dorsey in 1976.
(Author's collection)

George Beverly Shea.
(Courtesy Billy Graham Evangelistic Association)

Apollo released it on a two-sided 78-rpm record and in the first year Mahalia earned some $300,000 in royalties on it.

Author Langston Hughes, in his *Famous Negro Music Makers,* said of the recording: "It's slow, syncopated rhythm caught the fancy of jazz fans ... who bought it, not for religious reasons, but as a fine example of a new kind of rhythmical Negro singing. The gospel song began to reach a public for whom it was not intended at all ..."

She continued to record for Apollo Records but with a growing dissatisfaction for her deal there. As it turned out, the release of her records in Europe, where they drew lavish reviews, was what brought the greatest attention to her in the United States. In 1950, capitalizing on that European-stimulated public awareness of her, she appeared for the first time in New York's Carnegie Hall. It was a sellout performance, repeated again the following year.

In 1952, answering a genuine clamor for her presence, she toured Europe, booked into concert halls in England, France, Denmark, and Bethlehem in the Holy Land. The tour was a major success, topped by a smashing sale of her recording of "Silent Night" in Denmark.

Mahalia Jackson had arrived at the threshold of superstardom—a goal she had always sought. Her success, however, was not without cost: there were two failed marriages during the journey, some friends were lost as well, and she had garnered a reputation of being a difficult person with which to work. Indeed, she seemed to trust no one. Concert promoters across the land knew she expected to be paid her fee up front; she carried large sums of money in her copious brassiere.

If she needed verification of her stardom, she got it from Columbia Records, when that company's impresario, Mitch Miller, offered her a contract that would solidify her position as "Queen of Gospel." For months she carried the contract around with her in her large purse, agonizing over the small print. But she did sign it eventually—in 1953—opening up a whole new world for her.

Miller moved quickly to have broadcast producer Lou Cowan create a half-hour CBS radio show for her, to originate weekly out of Chicago. Beginning in September of 1954, the show had an audience but it never corralled a sponsor. In truth, she was on the air in the days when black artists simply were *not* given their own network shows. The other side of the coin was that advertising agencies weren't yet ready to sponsor programs headlining black performers. But it ran seventeen weeks on the CBS radio network as a half-hour show and then was suddenly cut to ten minutes. The handwriting was on the wall. After three more weeks of struggling with the demeaning ten-minute format, Mahalia ended the experiment.

Her hurt over the radio network's rejection was considerably assuaged by Mitch Miller's handling of her talents at Columbia Records. Album after album was released: *Mahalia Jackson, Sweet Little Jesus Boy, Bless This House, The World's Greatest Gospel Singer,* among them. Also an album titled *The Power and the Glory,* with the big Percy Faith orchestra, in which there were no "gospel songs" at all but, rather, hymns and anthems. Gospel music purists began to grumble. One critic complained that Columbia Records was turning Mahalia into "a black Kate Smith."

Nevertheless, she continued to grow in professional stature. Her appearances on network television were frequent, ranging from such shows as "Arthur Godfrey and His Friends" to "The Dinah Shore Show" to

"Night Beat." But she was not offered her own television show.

In 1956, she had her sixth annual Carnegie Hall concert, again with the SRO sign displayed in the box office. The music critic of the *New York Herald Tribune* wrote: ". . . her contralto voice had great range and expressiveness. It is ideally suited to . . . the gospel singer's specialized art—the falsetto highs and the rumbling lows, the whispered calms and the strident, shouting climaxes. . . . She has much of that belting show business style of delivery associated with Judy Garland and Al Jolson."

The following spring she had a major concert at Manhattan's prestigious Town Hall. Of that performance *Musical Americana* reported: "Here is a woman unafraid to express her faith without restraint and in her own individual manner."

In July of 1957 she was at the Newport, Rhode Island, Jazz Festival. The *New Yorker* music critic Whitney Balliett wrote that she performed with "an unforgettable eloquence and honesty . . ." A year later she was back at Newport to join with the Duke Ellington band in his gospel interlude, *Black, Brown and Beige.* It was another triumph.

Once again there were critics who said she had got away from her pure gospel roots. She ignored them, knowing she had remained true to her heritage.

"She never forgot her oldest and purist audiences," music journalist George T. Simon would write, "and more than once, after having earned something like $10,000 a night from a concert promoter, she would show up the next night in some small-town church and sing for free."

Few could go unstirred when listening to Mahalia Jackson. She had *earned* the title of "Queen of Gospel," and many considered that she was the principal reason for the popularization of gospel songs in the fifties and sixties.

Mahalia recognized—perhaps earlier than some—that she had made her way to the top of the heap. She had made a great deal of money, not only from her singing but from real estate and other investments in such enterprises as "Mahalia's Beauty Shop," "Mahalia's Flower Shop," and "Mahalia's Chicken Dinners." (In an appearance on NBC's "Tonight Show" she told host Johnny Carson: "The Colonel calls his food finger-lickin' good. I say mine is *tongue*-lickin' good.") And with fame and the money came responsibility; she understood that her voice raised in the civil rights struggle would have real impact.

Thus, when black seamstress Rosa Parks's refusal to go to the "back of the bus" in Montgomery, Alabama, in 1955, led to her arrest and started the headline-grabbing Birmingham Bus Boycott that was to catapult a young minister named Martin Luther King, Jr., to national prominence, Mahalia joined in the fight.

She went to Montgomery to sing at the St. John A. M. E. Church as a fund-raiser for the boycott. It was an all-night concert and she was at her best in a program that included "I've Heard of a City Called Heaven," "All to Jesus, I Surrender," "I'm Made Over," "God Is So Good to Me," her trademark "Move On Up a Little Higher" and then, because the Christmas season was approaching, "Silent Night, Holy Night."

As a black youngster born in the Deep South, Mahalia knew about segregation and racism. In 1957 it was to be brought home to her in Chicago. She had bought a house on Indiana Avenue in what was a predominantly white neighborhood on the city's south side. Not long after she moved in someone—never identified—fired air-rifle pellets into her living room windows. The warning was clear: she had invaded white turf and there were some who didn't want her there.

Edward R. Murrow, the literal icon of the early days of television news, was incensed by the act and the growing racism in the nation, and he offered to bring his CBS "Person to Person" interview show into Mahalia's home. She agreed.

Years later, in a conversation with writer Jules Schwerin, she would recall the happy ending of the story: "A group of people came to my door and asked if there was anything they could do to help. I said I would love to have all the children they could find. I wanted them with me on the TV show. Their mothers dressed them up, white and colored children, and they all came and we had a wonderful time. I cooked up a Louisiana Everything Gumbo—red beans and rice, ham and shrimp. We all ate together in my crowded kitchen—the cameramen, the children, neighbors, just everybody!"

But all was not well in the nation. Just three months after what might be regarded as the triumph of the civil rights March On Washington, President John F. Kennedy was assassinated in Dallas. In February of 1965, black leader Malcolm X was shot to death in Harlem. And on April 4, 1969, the Reverend Martin Luther King, Jr., was assassinated in Memphis.

Mahalia's ironbound faith was sorely tested. "America," she cried when she heard of King's death, "what have we become?"

No one had a ready answer.

The last years of Mahalia's Jackson's life—steeped in the emotionally hard work of performing and a gigantic appetite that fueled her massive body—were marked by declining health. Episodes of illness which intruded on her heavy singing schedule became more frequent. Then, on January 27, 1972, she died of a heart attack in the Little Company of Mary Hospital in Evergreen Park, Illinois. She was only sixty.

As might have been expected, there was a massive outpouring of grief in the City of Chicago. Thousands of mourners waited in the cold and snowy streets outside the Greater Salem Baptist Church, where she had spent forty years as a member of the choir, to pay their last respects. When thousands were still left outside when the announced period of mourning ended, Mayor Richard Daley stepped in and announced that the memorial service would be extended another day, with Mahalia's body lying in state at the large Aerie Crown Theatre at McCormick Place, Lake Shore Drive.

Ten thousand passed her bier at that location. And there were eulogies aplenty.

Coretta King, widow of Martin: "She was black and proud and beautiful. . . . A woman with extraordinary gifts as a singer, singing songs of her people. She was my friend and she was a friend of mankind."

Reverend Jesse Jackson: "I give thanks to God for letting Mahalia come this way."

Jazz singer Ella Fitzgerald: "This great woman is now gone from us. I tell you, there's not another singer like her in the world!'

Aretha Franklin sang "Precious Lord, Take My Hand," composed by Mahalia's mentor, Thomas A. Dorsey.

When the emotion-packed day was ended, the body was flown to New Orleans. There the grieving started all over again. Mourners jammed the New Orleans airport, and thousands more lined the streets as the cortege slowly made its way from the airport into the city and through the black "inner city," hard by the Mississippi River docks where her father had worked.

The casket was taken to the giant Rivergate convention hall where eight thousand fought their way inside for special services, which included a five-hundred-voice citywide choir.

Again, the eulogies. President Richard Nixon sent a message: "The spirit of Mahalia Jackson will stir in the soul of our country the resolute will to press forward in achieving the true meaning of brotherhood to which she gave such a poignant and dynamic voice."

Actor Harry Belafonte spoke: "She was the single most powerful black woman in the United States, the woman-power for the grass roots. There is not a single fieldhand, a single black worker, a single black intellectual who did not respond to her civil rights message."

There followed a twelve-mile cortege to the Providence Memorial Park in Metairie, a New Orleans suburb, followed by marching bands playing dirges. After a brief commitment service, the bands, traditionally now playing hand-clapping gospel songs and Dixieland swing, led the throng back to the streets of the "Big Easy."

It was remembered by some that, in her later years, she had been opportuned to sing in night clubs, to be a "blues singer." More than a few Las Vegas entrepreneurs had offered her major-money deals. She always turned them down.

"I have many fine friends," she said, "who entertain in night clubs and theaters, but it's not the place for my kind of singing. I don't work for money. I sing because I love to sing.

"I try to sing the way I *feel,* and most of the time I feel good."

7

George Beverly Shea

"ONE OF THE CHARACTERISTICS THAT MAKES BEV SHEA unique as a singer," evangelist Billy Graham has said, "is that he sings a sermon. Many other singers are more spectacular, but he is in a class by himself when it comes to worshipful singing. His walk with God has been sincere; he really means what he sings."

Reverend Graham ought to know, for the evangelist and the singer have been colleagues for half a century— an association more expansive than other storied evangelistic pairings: Dwight Moody–Ira Sankey or Billy Sunday–Homer Rodeheaver or Sam James–E. O. Excell, for example.

Perhaps the hallmark of George Beverly Shea over the years has been his *consistency,* both in the living of his life and in his singing. Without question, time has taken its toll on his marvelous bass-baritone voice—yet it remains capable of spiritually moving the thousands who attend the Graham Crusades and the millions more who see them on television.

Shea has had a singing career that would clearly signal "stardom" in the world of secular music. He has had long associations with several network radio programs, and has been a multimillion album seller at RCA Records, releasing sixty-four albums since 1951. All of that career has been built on his faith.

There were opportunities to have a secular career. But in the final analysis, to bring it down to a single point, secular stardom rested on the word "hell."

In the midst of the Great Depression, a friend and fellow singer called to Bev's attention that the noted choral director of the day, Lynn Murray, was holding auditions at the CBS radio network in New York. The year was 1936; young Shea was married and had a $34.50-a-week job as a clerk in the medical department of the Mutual of New York (MONY) Life Insurance Company. Being a Lynn Murray singer offered something more substantial, at least $75 a week.

At the audition, Bev sang "Swanee River" and then "Down to the River" when Murray asked for a second song. What happened then was recalled by Shea in his biography, *Then Sings My Soul:*

"After I had finished my second 'river' number, Mr. Murray nodded approvingly and handed me a piece of music ('Song of the Vagabonds' from Rudolph Friml's *The Vagabond King*), which they were going to sing at the Texas Centennial. Included in its libretto, I discovered, was a line which made me feel uncomfortable. It read, '. . . and to hell with Burgundy . . .'

" 'I want you to learn this right away,' Mr. Murray said. 'We'll be in touch.'

"I took the music and wandered out of the studio in somewhat of a daze. My thoughts were all confused. I had won, but lost. Mr. Murray seemed impressed, but what if he really offered me a job? Could I take it and sing a line such as '. . . to hell with Burgundy'? If I did, what would be the next compromise?"

Lynn Murray did offer Bev Shea a job, not once but twice. The young man, after giving it prayerful consideration, turned down the offer. In 1990s terms, making a career decision on the basis of having to sing one line with a swear word in it, may seem hopelessly naive. But in 1936 that was Shea's decision; in 1994 it would be the same.

That has been George Beverly Shea over more than eighty years: *constant* in his beliefs.

He was born on February 1, 1909, the fourth child of Adam J. and Maude (Whitney) Shea, in Winchester, Ontario, Canada. His father was a Methodist minister; his mother was a minister's daughter, who was a singer and a musician.

"One of the earliest memories I have," Bev Shea would write, "is that of my mother singing this verse:

> *Singing I go along life's road,*
> *Praising the Lord, praising the Lord,*
> *Singing I go along life's road,*
> *For Jesus has lifted my load.*

"Not a morning went by—not a weekday morning—but what I would be awakened by a heavy chord from the piano followed by Mother's sweet soprano voice."

Under his mother's tutelage, the young boy learned to play the piano. Everything musical, including a mouth organ his mother bought for him, intrigued Bev; he also learned to play his father's violin. As a seventeen-year-old, he sang in public for the first time at a Methodist camp meeting. And a year later he came forward in his father's church to dedicate his life to Christ.

After a year at Houghton College in New York State, Bev moved to New Jersey with his family when his father accepted a pastorate in Jersey City. It was then that he got a job at MONY in Manhattan. That was just two months before the stock market crash of 1929.

As a singer, Bev found numerous opportunities in the New York City area. He sang, for example, on comedian Fred Allen's amateur talent show on the NBC radio network, earning $15 for his rendition of "Go Down Moses." In addition to singing regularly in the choir of his father's church, he also sang on a radio ministry program on WKBO, Jersey City, and with a gospel quartet on "Meditations on the Psalms" on WHN and WMCA, New York. And all the while he maintained a voluminous correspondence with his long-time sweetheart, Erma Scharfe, in Canada.

In June of 1934, Bev and Erma married, moving into a small studio apartment in Fort Lee, New Jersey, from which he would commute to his job at the insurance company in Manhattan. He continued to sing from time to time on New York radio stations and at summer Bible conferences, but none of that was lucrative. He even recorded for Decca Records's Jack Kapp, who cut two 78-rpm records of Bev singing "Jesus Whispers Peace," "Lead Me Gently Home, Father," "I'd Rather Have Jesus," and "God Understands." But no continuing contract with Decca came out of that effort.

It was at about that time that Shea was offered the regular position with the famous Lynn Murray Singers, confident that he had made the proper decision in refusing it and believing something else would come along. And so it did. A family friend, the Reverend Dr. Will Houghton, then president of the Moody Bible Institute in Chicago, offered him a staff position on the Moody radio station, WMBI. Bev accepted in August of 1938, moving to the Windy City.

Initially he sang on Dr. Houghton's weekly program, "Let's Go Back to the Bible," which originated on

WMBI for a small network of stations. By March of 1939 he became a staff announcer on WMBI, hosting a morning program called "Hymns from the Chapel." His mother's "Singing I Go" was Bev's theme song.

"Apparently the program had a few followers at neighboring Wheaton College," Shea wrote. "I remember one day in 1943—a young man from Wheaton stopped by the studio to introduce himself. He was a tall, rather thin fellow with a shock of blond hair and a delightful smile.

" 'We listen to your program each morning, Mr. Shea,' he said. 'I really enjoy it.'

" 'Well, I appreciate that,' I replied and asked about his schooling and his plans. He told me he was a student pastor at the Christian Missionary Alliance Church in Wheaton and hoped to get into evangelistic work. After a few minutes of pleasant conversation, he departed with 'I hope to see you again, Mr. Shea.'

" 'Sure thing,' I answered."

Thus did Bev Shea meet Billy Graham; there was nothing in the meeting to presage a future association.

In June of 1944 Shea left Moody's noncommercial WMBI to host a commercially sponsored religious music program on Chicago's WCFL. The sponsor was Club Aluminum (cooking ware); the title of the daily fifteen-minute show was "Club Time." It did so well that in September of 1945 it was moved to the ABC radio network, where it became a fixture for the next seven years.

There was another religious program on WCFL at the time, titled "Songs in the Night," hosted by Christian broadcaster Torrey Johnson. His other commitments— preaching and teaching—made his continuation of the program impossible. Johnson offered it to Billy Graham, then the pastor of The Village Church in Western Springs, Illinois, about twenty miles southwest of Chicago. The little church congregation, however, could not afford the $100 a week it would cost to keep the program on the air. Pastor Graham, recognizing the value of a full-time radio pulpit, gave up his $45-a-week salary to the project; the church deacons added the rest.

Billy Graham remembers: "I was determined to get George Beverly Shea as my singer. This was like reaching for the moon but, after a great deal of prayer, I went in fear and trembling to ask if he would come and sing—at least on the opening program."

"How he [Graham] enjoys telling about that visit," Bev wrote in his autobiography. " 'I had to go through three secretaries,' he begins. 'The last one said Mr. Shea was preparing his program and could not possibly be disturbed. I turned to go, but something stopped me. Instead of walking through the door that led to the street, I walked through the door which said "Beverly Shea" in big, bold letters.'

"About the only thing I will vouch for in this story is the fact that they had my name on the door—in decal letters that you buy at Woolworth's . . ."

Whatever the details of the meeting, it ended with Graham persuading Shea to sing regularly on his "Songs in the Night," while continuing on the commercial "Club Time."

"We have been colleagues in evangelism," Graham says, "ever since that spring day in 1944."

"It was the beginning," Bev Shea says, "—the humble beginning—of an unbelievable journey."

The journey, it can be argued, really didn't get started in full until 1947, after Graham and song leader Cliff Barrows had returned from a *Youth for Christ* evangelistic tour of the British Isles: six months, twenty-seven cities, 360 meetings.

Graham wrote to Shea (from North Carolina) in May of 1947 of the success of the English meetings, commenting on the fact that evangelism meant specifically for young people also drew parents and grandparents in large numbers. "There is a feeling among some of us," Billy said, "that we should go back again some day and hold a campaign not directed primarily at youth. We have received similar requests here in the States. Right now my thoughts are turning to a three-week, city-wide rally scheduled for November in Charlotte."

Billy reported that he had recruited Cliff Barrows as song leader, his old schoolmate, the Reverend Grady Wilson, as associate pastor, and that he wanted Shea as soloist. "I am convinced," Graham wrote, "the Lord wants you to be our soloist in these upcoming meetings."

Even from the beginning, then, of what came to be called the Graham Crusades, the pattern was somewhat different from earlier major evangelistic organizations. With both the Dwight Moody and Billy Sunday campaigns, for example, the principal musical personalities—Ira Sankey and Homer Rodeheaver—were song leader, choir director, and soloist all rolled into one. With Graham he was turning song leader duties to Barrows and bringing Bev Shea aboard as featured soloist; although all would deny it, Bev was given the star role. He was, after all, a nationally known Christian singer, already popular because of his network radio show.

The first number performed by Shea at the Charlotte meetings was "I Will Sing the Wondrous Story," one of Graham's favorites. The newfound evangelistic team—Graham, Wilson, Shea, and Barrows—conducted services for two weeks in the packed First Baptist Church and then had to move to the Charlotte Armory to accomodate the growing crowds.

Not all of the early evangelistic efforts met with such success. There was a worrisome period that Shea would later describe as a time for "finding our groove." And perhaps the real groove was found in Los Angeles in the latter part of 1949. A local group, mostly laymen, invited Graham and his team to come to L. A. for a three-week campaign. A huge tent was pitched at the corner of Washington Boulevard and Hill Street and was soon dubbed the "Canvas Cathedral."

Some six thousand crowded into the tent each night and many hundreds of those came forward during every meeting to accept Christ. The question was asked: Should the campaign be extended beyond the planned three weeks? Graham was hesitant, praying for some tangible sign that the meetings should continue.

The sign came in the person of Stuart Hamblen, Los Angeles's most prominent radio personality for a period of more than fifteen years. "Cowboy" singing star, songwriter of note, and a Hollywood legend of sorts, Hamblen was a consummate hell-raiser. He was well known to the police of Los Angeles and was frequently arrested for anything from fistfights to shooting out street lights to just general public drunkenness.

Urged on by his wife Suzy, for whom he had written many love songs, Hamblen came forward one evening in the "Canvas Cathedral," publicly confessed his sins, and accepted Christ as his saviour. Stuart was so well known in the area that the story of his being "born again" was headline news. He himself told the story, and retold it, on his radio show and newspapers carried feature stories on the conversion of the profligate "cowboy."

On the basis of the reaction to Hamblen's experience, the "Christ for Greater Los Angeles" campaign was extended for another week and then another. In all, it would continue for eight weeks, helped along by a terse memo to his publications by newspaper-magazine tycoon William Randolph Hearst. It said: "Puff Graham." Hearst's editors did just that.

As it was to turn out, Stuart Hamblen's conversion was a genuine, lasting one. In the months following he wrote his most beautiful love song for Suzy: "(Remember Me?) I'm the One Who Loves You." And shortly thereafter he wrote his most important gospel song, "It Is No Secret (What God Can Do)."

Hamblen told Nashville music columnist Robert K. Oermann how that song came to be written. "The Hamblens lived in the old Errol Flynn mansion," Oermann reported, "next door to John Wayne. When Wayne threw a party celebrating the completion of [the film] *Red River,* the guests were all talking about psychiatry, which was then becoming the rage. Hamblen said he didn't think a psychiatrist could do any more for a person than a little prayer could: 'After all, it's no secret what God can do in your life.' And Wayne said, 'You oughta write a song called that.'

"Back home, Hamblen sat alone downstairs while Suzy put her hair in curlers, getting ready for bed. 'It was midnight when I sat down at the organ,' he said. 'Exactly seventeen minutes later I looked up at the clock and my wife came downstairs to see what I'd been doing. I played the song for her. She started crying and said, 'Mark my word, that'll be sung around the world.' "

Mrs. Hamblen was correct. "It Is No Secret" has been recorded more than three hundred times, in many languages.

Hamblen was to have a plethora of good gospel songs—"Open Up Your Heart (And Let the Sunshine In)," "The Lord is Counting on You," "He Bought My Soul At Calvary," "Army of the Lord," "Help Thou My Unbelief," "These Things Shall Pass," "My

Religion's Not Old Fashioned,'' "One Day Nearer Home,'' to mention only a few.

Then, in 1954, there was "This Old House.''

Hamblen made a recording comeback of sorts to cut it for RCA Victor, selling about five hundred thousand copies. Not bad. But it was Rosemary Clooney's pop-novelty version that was the monster hit, and the songwriter didn't like it at all.

"I wanted Bing Crosby to record it, but he needed a priest to bless it first,'' Hamblen chuckled. "Rosemary Clooney was standing there and said, 'Well, I'll take it right now.' When I heard her version of it I threw it on the ground and stomped on it. Four million records sold later. I've decided I love her version, and God bless that woman!''

Stuart Hamblen's conversion and Bev Shea's growing friendship with him led directly to Shea's long-standing recording contract with RCA Victor. It all began when Hamblen asked Bev to make an evangelistic appearance with him at Philadelphia's Convention Hall. In the audience that night was an RCA Victor representative—there at Hamblen's insistence—who carried back to his home office a glowing report on Shea's performance.

Within weeks a contract was offered to him; Bev sought Billy Graham's approval and got it: "Bev, that's wonderful! What an opportunity. Why, with records you'll be able to witness all over the world, night and day.''

From the first recording it was clear that RCA Victor intended for George Beverly Shea to be one of its principal artists. His first album, recorded in the spring of 1951, featured the lush Hugo Winterhalter Orchestra and was produced by Victor's top man, Stephen H. Sholes. The album was titled *Inspirational Songs* and would become known at RCA as "Old Faithful Number

1187." (A full-page advertisement in an October, 1968, issue of *Billboard*, the show business journal, still featured Shea's *Inspiration Songs* album, more than fifteen years after its initial release.)

That first album included such songs as "Ivory Palaces," "Known Only to Him," "Tenderly He Watches," "If You Know the Lord," and Stuart Hamblen's "It Is No Secret (What God Can Do)."

The close association of Shea and Sholes would lead to the recording executive's conversion at a Graham Crusade in Pittsburgh. Early in 1968, Bev flew to New York to attend a testimonial luncheon honoring Sholes. The day after that luncheon, Shea and Sholes met to listen to some Ralph Carmichael-arranged songs for their next album, to be titled *Be Still My Soul*. One of the selections was Fanny Crosby's gospel standard, "Safe In the Arms of Jesus." Sholes smiled when he heard it: "Bev, those words mean so much to me—now."

Just a few weeks later—in the latter part of April—Shea received a cable in Sydney, Australia, where he had gone with the Graham Crusade, informing him of Sholes's death. A principal figure in the establishment of Nashville, Tennessee, as "Music City U. S. A.," Steve had flown there to attend a meeting of the Country Music Foundation, rented a car at the airport, and was driving to Music Row when he suffered a fatal heart attack.

Sholes had already introduced Bev Shea to the wonders of the "Nashville Sound." Danny Davis, known for his innovative "Nashville Brass," produced a number of albums with Shea, on which Bill Walker, former musical director for country music legend Eddy Arnold, was the arranger and conductor.

Shea's RCA albums were consistently big sellers: *Whispering Hope, Be Still My Soul, Crossroads of Life,*

Southland Favorites (with The Anita Kerr Singers), Evening Vespers, Hymns That Have Lived 100 Years, The King Is Coming, Surely Goodness and Mercy (with The Blackwood Brothers Quartet), Hallelujah, and fifty-five other albums.

Bev Shea's need to find the best gospel songs for his albums and his thousands of appearances with the Billy Graham Crusades around the world honed his already healthy appreciation of the men and women who wrote the hymns and gospel songs. That appreciation led to a second book (*Songs That Lift the Heart*), in which he offered inspirational stories of the creation of some of the world's greatest Christian songs.

Key among them was the story of "How Great Thou Art," which was to play a major role in Shea's life. While in London in 1954, the head of a British religious book publishing house brought the song to Bev's attention, giving him a leaflet of it. It was not a new piece; it was almost seventy years old when Shea first saw it and it had a unique and circuitous story.

It was written in Sweden in 1885 or 1886 by the Reverend Carl Boberg, a noted preacher and religious editor. The original title was "O Store Gud" ("O Great God"). It was translated from Swedish to German in 1907 and then into Russian in 1912. Oddly, it was published *in Russian* in 1922 by the American Bible Society in New York City, and included in a large hymnal in 1927. (In the meantime there was a first translation into English in 1925, with the title changed to "O Mighty God.") However, the 1927 hymnal came into the hands of Stuart K. Hine, a missionary in the Ukraine.

Hine translated the first three verses from Russian to English, added a fourth verse, retitled it "How Great Thou Art," and had some leaflets printed of his work.

It was one of those leaflets that had been given to Bev Shea.

"The song was packed away among my things," Shea wrote. "One day I was sorting through some notes and came across the leaflet. . . . Sitting down at the piano, I played and sang it through:

O Lord my God, when I in awesome wonder
    Consider all the world Thy hands have made,
I see the stars, I hear the rolling thunder,
    Thy power throughout the Universe displayed.

When Christ shall come with shout of acclamation
    And take me home, what joy shall fill my heart!
Then I shall bow in humble adoration,
    And there proclaim, my God, how great Thou art!

Then sings my soul, my Savior God to Thee:
    How great Thou art, how great Thou Art!
Then sings my soul, my Savior God to Thee:
    How great Thou art, how great Thou Art!

"It was beautiful.

"I couldn't wait to do it in a Crusade and mentioned 'How Great Thou Art' to Cliff (Barrows) the next time we were together. His face brightened because he had played it over himself and shared my enthusiasm. It was sung for the first time at Maple Leaf Garden in 1955, during the Toronto Crusade.

"The response was unbelievable. . . . After the Toronto Crusade and its *Hour of Decision* exposure, its popularity spread across the country with such frenzy that it soon became one of the most popular hymns in America."

At the great 1957 Crusade in New York's Madison Square Garden—sixteen weeks, total attendance two million—Shea sang "How Great Thou Art" with a two-thousand-voice choir a total of ninety-nine times! He would ultimately record it for three different RCA Victor albums. Hardly a personal appearance goes by without him singing it.

Of course, Shea has been a writer of gospel songs himself, including one titled "I'd Rather Have Jesus," composed when he was only twenty years old, written to a poem by Rhea F. Miller. It would sell more than one million pieces of sheet music, Shea modestly giving all the credit to the lyricist for its popularity.

That modesty pervades everything Bev does. In 1955, when he was on the way to Britain aboard the SS *United States*, a fellow passenger asked him what happened at the Graham Crusades. "I found myself at a loss for words," Shea wrote, "when I tried to describe the response that usually accompanied Mr. Graham's invitation to become a Christian: 'What happens then never becomes commonplace ... watching people by the hundreds coming forward ... of, if you could just see the wonder of it all.' "

The passenger, impressed with Shea's emotion on the subject, wrote the words THE WONDER OF IT ALL on a card, handed it to Bev and suggested, "That sounds like a song to me."

That very night in his cabin, Shea wrote lyrics on the theme and roughed out a melody. He wasn't too impressed with it; he was having trouble with a rhyme:

The wonder of sunset at evening,
The wonder of sunrise at morn,
But the wonder of wonders that thrills my soul,
Is the wonder that God loves me.

Eventually, Bev turned to an old friend, Texas song-writer Cindy Walker, a prolific producer of country music hits, for help with the lyrics. "Inside of a minute" (Bev's words), Cindy had the answer, changing two words in the second line:

> *The wonder of sunset at evening,*
> *The wonder of sunrise* I see . . .

"And that's how it was published," he said, "thanks to a real songwriter, Cindy Walker!"

If one accepts the contention that Shea is not a "real songwriter," then Bev will have to accept the revelation that there are hundreds of "real songwriters" out there who would give their right arms to have George Beverly Shea sing their songs.

He has long been in a class by himself.

8

Bill and Gloria Gaither

IF THERE HAS BEEN A TRANSITIONAL FORCE IN AMERICAN gospel music between what is known as the southern gospel tradition and today's compact disc/videocassette generation of gospel performers—between the old and the new—then it must be headquartered in the small Indiana town of Alexandria and be strongly in the hands and hearts of two former English teachers: Bill and Gloria Gaither.

For there in Alexandria, just a few miles west of Interstate 69 and less than a hundred miles north of Indianapolis, the Gaithers, husband and wife, have been both the catalysts of the new and gracious stewards of the old. By the accident of years they seem to be perfectly positioned between the two and have been able to promote and appreciate both.

They have a real modesty about their roles in gospel music, but they are realistically honest about what those roles have been.

"If we are called to anything," Bill said quietly, "we have always felt that there are more things that unite us within the body of Christ than divide us.'' He chuckled. ''We didn't sit down when we were twenty years old and say, 'Be a bridge now.' But looking back on thirty years in Christian music, I think we were strongly motivated to say to the person on the right-wing extreme of theology and to the person on the left-wing extreme of theology ... to say to both of them, 'I think if we could get together over a cup of coffee, you'd really like each other.'

''I think it's sad that within the Christian church we segregate many other ways than just racially. We segregate socially and economically. We segregate, especially, age-wise. And when it comes to music, if you want to divide a family real fast ... the guy who said, 'Music is the universal language,' lied at that point, because *styles* do divide people.''

Gloria added: ''I'm not sure that the Christian community, historically and even now, can tell the difference between substance and form. If you want to divide believers real quick, they'll be divided on the issue of form. ... Maybe the one way we can unite is on *substance*. And I guess that's another thing we felt called to do ... to bring people together, whatever the style, whatever the form, and say, 'Does it have any substance; is there any eternity in it?' ... The thing that can unite us is to change the focus—from form to substance.''

That's exactly what Bill and Gloria Gaither have attempted to do (and one can argue that they have done it successfully) in their Pinebrook Recording Studios in Alexandria, Indiana. There they have brought together the diverse forms of gospel music—and the diverse generations—and have concentrated on the substance of Christian faith. The medium has been the production of a series of videocassettes, a spontaneous melding of musical styles.

The videos, titled "Homecoming," "Reunion," "Turn Your Radio On," and "Old Friends," have brought together such legends of gospel music as James Blackwood, the Florida Boys, Vestal and Howard Goodman, Eva Mae LeFevre, Doug Oldham, The Speers, Hovie and Mosie Lister (and more), with such contemporary standouts as Cynthia Clawson, Michael English, Mark Lowry, Gary McSpadden, Mylon LeFevre, the Gaithers themselves (and more).

They sang together, laughed together, cried together, and glorified the Lord together in an emotional outpouring of faith so overwhelming that it needed the discipline of music to contain it.

There will be more videos to come; new titles will be "The Old Landmark" and "Precious Memories." Also there will be a video bringing together some 150 black gospel legends, including Billy Preston, Jennifer Holiday, the Old Clara Ward Singers, the Harmonettes, the Barrett Sisters, and, inevitably, more.

Bill Gaither grew up in the rural-oriented Alexandria, an admitted "weird kid" who had an obsession with music, dreaming of becoming a gospel singer. His mother, encouraging him, taped gospel music quartets on the radio while Bill was in school so that he could listen to the latest songs when he came home. Just out of high school, he started a gospel quartet. It was *not* a success.

So he worked his way through nearby Anderson College (now Anderson University), earning a teaching degree in English in 1959; in 1961 he had a master's degree in guidance from Ball State University. When the opportunity came to teach English at his old high school, he seized upon it.

On his first day on the job he met one Gloria Sickal, a substitute teacher of French who was still a junior at

Anderson College. Was it fate? "People say that opposites attract," Bill says. "In our case it was the likenesses that pulled us together. The draw was philosophical; it also helped that she was pretty."

Gloria was a PK (a preacher's kid) from Michigan. She was maintaining a triple major at Anderson College—French, Sociology, and English. "I only knew," Gloria explains, "that I wanted to be somehow involved in full-time Christian work. But there weren't many careers available to women in the church. You could either marry a minister, become a foreign missionary or teach." Not sure where she was headed, the triple major was a hedge on any of those ultimate decisions.

Then she met Bill Gaither; they were married in 1962. The following year Gloria graduated, *cum laude,* from college. They continued to teach at Alexandria High School for a time until they started a family— daughter Suzanne was born in 1964—and until Bill's growing success as a Christian songwriter completely changed their directions.

A musical ministry was clearly under way. On weekends, Bill, his brother, Danny, and his sister, Mary Ann, played the church supper circuit in Indiana as a singing act. It was inevitable, it seems in hindsight, that Gloria would start to work with Bill on his songs, gradually contributing more and more of the lyrics, and would become the third member of what was billed as "The Gaither Trio."

"When I was a little girl," she laughed, "the *last* thing I ever dreamed of becoming was a gospel singer." But the act prospered.

"We always had a lot of confidence in our songs; we thought they were pretty good," Bill recalled. "We didn't have the same confidence in our performing. We knew we were limited vocally. It didn't make any difference. We started at churches and pretty soon churches couldn't hold it. So we started going to high school auditoriums, a thousand seats, and selling tickets, and pretty soon that wouldn't hold it, so we then went to city auditoriums with 2,500 seats.''

In 1969, lightning struck. Bill's composition, ''He Touched Me,'' was nominated for a Grammy Award and, in the first year of the Dove Awards given by the Gospel Music Association, Gaither was named the ''Songwriter of the Year.'' It wasn't until 1978 that someone other than Bill Gaither would be given the Dove as the GMA's ''Songwriter of the Year.'' (In 1986, Gloria Gaither would be named ''Songwriter of the Year'' in her own right.)

Also in 1969, the contemporary gospel quartet, the Imperials, largely on the strength of their sensational recording of ''He Touched Me,'' won the Dove as ''Group of the Year.''

Gaither remembers: ''The Imperials were backing Elvis Presley on one of his road shows and he would have them do one song a night and they would sing 'He Touched Me.' Elvis heard it so many times he said, 'I want to record that in my next gospel album.' So he did and titled the album, *He Touched Me* and it won a Grammy. And Elvis not only wanted to sing the lead, but when they went up four steps and the tenor took the lead, he wanted to do that, too. When the tenor went up to B-flat, Elvis also wanted to do that. I don't know whether he could hit B-flat, but he thought he could and went up and tried it. But Elvis just basically took the Imperials's arrangement, because that was a classic arrangement, written by Henry Slaughter.''

''He Touched Me'' was covered by dozens of performers, including many of the prominent country music singers, as well as the likes of Kate Smith and even Jimmy Durante.

"A song like that," Gaither added, "is just born out of the mystical presence of Christ. A change in your life. There's still nothing as touching or as moving as the first-person testimony of someone coming forward and saying, 'I was a drug addict. I had no hope. I was down. Then the hand of Jesus touched me.' That is the essence of the gospel: changing lives. And that will never get old."

To put a sum to it, "He Touched Me" took Bill Gaither to the top of the gospel music field. The year 1969 was special, also, because Bill and Gloria became parents of a second daughter, Amy; in 1970, son Benjamin was born.

With it all, the demands grew for the Gaither Trio. They moved now from the 2,500-seat municipal auditoriums to the ten-thousand-seat arenas. It was a difficult transition.

"We may have been the first ones in our field to do the arenas," Bill said, "but we didn't have the public address equipment to handle them and we had to feel our way there. We probably lost something when we went into the arenas, because ours was more of a one-on-one kind of thing. It was all simply an outgrowth of our writing and who we were on the inside."

Brother Danny was with the trio for nearly thirteen years. When he left the road in 1976, he was replaced by Gary McSpadden, who stayed for a decade before leaving to pursue a solo career. Then came young Michael English in 1986, who is still with the trio even though he, too, has a successful solo career now. English was the Dove Award-winning "New Artist of 1992."

Before McSpadden left the trio, however, he was part of what was perceived as a necessary expansion of the Gaither performing act—the establishment of a male quartet (long a staple of gospel music) called "The

Gaither Vocal Band.'' The original group included McSpadden, Gaither, Steve Green, and Lee Young. Bill introduced the vocal band to a crowd of ten thousand in Florida in January of 1981, somewhat apologetically because he and the other three were going to try something ''new.''

They sang a song called ''First Day In Heaven,'' originally sung by The Statesmen in 1954. Their telling four-part harmony won immediate acceptance; there was a demand for an encore. But they had none. The group was so new that they had rehearsed only one number. So they simply sang ''First Day In Heaven'' again, once more to ringing applause.

There had been personnel changes in the vocal band, as with most quartets in the business. ''The Vocal Band,'' says Gaither, ''has always been made up of people who had other things going at the same time—Larnelle Harris, Steve Green, Gary McSpadden. It's made us able to get great singers who are so good that people say, 'I want to hear him as a solo.' It's also helped us maintain a freshness by allowing each of us to be involved in different projects. The Vocal Band helps the members' solo careers and the solo careers help the Vocal Band.''

The current roster of the quartet includes Gaither, English, Christian comic and singer Mark Lowry, and a young Terry Franklin, who has a musical ministry with his wife, Barbi, outside the confines of the Gaither Vocal Band. Both of the Franklins not only sing together but they are collaborative songwriters as well.

The Gaither Trio has recorded more than forty albums, selling into the millions. The quartet, of course, has fewer albums. However, those albums have pushed the envelope of Christian music a bit. On one hand, on *Southern Classics* (Benson), the singers have made a low bow to the more traditional aspect of gospel music.

And, on the other hand, their newest album, *Peace of the Rock* (Star Song), has been more contemporary.

One critic wrote: "Vocally the leanings are reminiscent of the early Eagles and Crosby, Stills, and Nash, with very little obvious help from Mr. Gaither. Some will miss his lead vocal work, while others will applaud his vision to let the kids watch the store. But the quality has Gaither all over it."

As for the kids watching the store, one of the cuts in the new album, "Arms Around the World," has lyrics written by Gaither daughter Suzanne Gaither-Jennings, and music by Bill, Terry, and Barbi Franklin, and the album's producer, Cheryl Rogers.

Over the years, then, Bill and Gloria Gaither have built at Alexandria what can honestly be regarded as a substantial gospel music conglomerate. Bill doesn't deny the use of that businesslike word, but he has a ready explanation for it all.

"Every business that we're in we were forced into," he said. "For this reason: a writer creates something and he wants it to go as far as he can make it go, because he believes in that idea. I don't care how great the marketing team is, how great the company is, nobody is going to believe in the idea like the creator believes in it. And in the very early days I saw people who were taking their God-given gifts and turning them over to somebody else who had a bunch of other food on their plate and I saw some wonderful food falling off the table. And I said to myself on the writing, 'We need to do our own thing.' Not because we wanted to build a conglomerate, not that we wanted to be big business moguls, but we think we can take the idea farther than assigning it to another company. So that started the Gaither Music Company.

"We started doing concerts," Bill went on, "and

we'd come to a town and the promoter had not only our concert, but ten other ones. And we'd say, 'What kind of crowd do you think we'll have?' And he'd say, 'Well, we've done a lot of publicity; we've really got the word out.' 'But how many people do you think are going to be there?' 'Well, I don't know.' We got tired of that and we finally said, 'You know something— when we leave the city limits and leave our three kids and get on a plane to go to Kansas City, go to Dallas, go to L.A., this is the only time we're going to go there this year. We want to talk to as many people as we can talk to when we get there.' So we started a promotion company called Spring House. We take the risks and spend the money necessary to build the biggest audience possible.

"The same thing happened with the Pinebrook Recording Studios. We got tired of getting into a car and driving to Nashville. It's six hours no matter how you look at it, and you're away from your family. It seems like every business we've got into we've been forced into it. And I've tried to stay away from any unrelated thing. But to stay with all of the related things to our gospel music. There's also the other side of me: I'm one artist who enjoys doing business. I don't mind that. I'm a teacher at heart and it's fun to take a staff and train them, and motivate them, and inspire them, and get things done at the level that I think it ought to be done."

That attention to detail has led to staggering successes at the Gaithers' operation in Alexandria, Indiana. Bill and Gloria have co-written some five hundred songs, there have been the multiple recordings, more concert appearances than can be counted, and honors aplenty—Bill was inducted into the Gospel Music Hall of Fame in 1982, they have garnered a shelf full of

Dove Awards from the GMA, there have been prestigious Grammy Awards, and chart-topping song hits.

"You know, when the records started to sell," Bill
said, "I didn't really know why. But I gave thanks that
it did happen. Then came the Doves and the Grammys
and I gave thanks again. I've often said that I've been
up for a bunch of them [the awards] and I never understood why I won them, just as I never understood it
when I didn't win them." He laughed heartily.

The creative process, of course, is what has fueled
the Alexandria machine.

"I guess every writer works in a different way,"
Gloria commented. "But with Bill and me it has always
begun with an idea—the concept of an idea that we've
been consumed with for a period of time. And we say,
'There ought to be a song there expressing that somehow.' Sometimes the words come first, sometimes the
music, but the idea is paramount. *Then* we look for the
musical setting that fits the idea.

"A good example of that is the song, 'I Am Loved.'
Basically, that just came from dealing with some pretty
difficult people. And we came to the conclusion that
the most nasty people are those who really don't believe
they're loved. You can slice that any way you want to,
but the little Sunday school song we all sang, 'Jesus
loves me, this I know,' could change the world if it
were universally believed.

"If one can really believe that the God of the Uni-
verse, who knows everything there is to know about
us, really loved that troubled individual, then it would
supercede all the abuse, or negative experiences of
childhood, or bad marriages, or whatever undermines
people's self-confidence and self-identity and makes
them nasty human beings. That all could be healed, I
really do believe, if we could show that it is God's
opinion of you ultimately is [*sic*] the one that matters

most. He says: 'You're valuable, you're loved.' And we asked, as songwriters, 'How can we turn that phrase so that the listener will hear it again?' The answer was the song, 'I Am Loved.'"

Bill and Gloria recognized that many idea concepts are manageable in one song, but that some ideas are too big to be expressed in a single song. As Gloria put it: "There needed to be ten nails driven into the board to hold the idea down."

Thus was born the Gaither musicals, performance pieces for choirs, based on a single concept, with several spoken narratives, and all-new music. Bill was quick to point out: "That idea really came out of our one-night concerts and from a friend of ours, the orchestrator Ronn Huff. The first one we did was a praise work called *Alleluia!*, which interestingly enough was the first certified gold album in our field. Ironically, we were only creating a work for choirs and we made a demo record for the choirs to guide them and show them what we had. And God has a weird sense of humor, because it caught on as a record-record and sold a million copies. As a matter of fact, it has now gone platinum."

That first musical was so successful that now there are ten, with more certainly to come. The musicals do not carry a performance fee, but choirs can obtain a complete package from the Gaither Music Company that includes a recording (compact disc or cassette), choral books, orchestrations, and, for choirs who don't have the availability of live musicians, there are recorded performance accompaniment tracks. Even rehearsal tracks for the singers.

One would think that with all they now do, Bill and Gloria Gaither couldn't find another minute for anything else. Not so. Bill has written a book of memoirs (with Jerry Jenkins) for Thomas Nelson Publishers in Nashville: *I Almost Missed the Sunset: My Perspective On Life and Music.* Gloria has been the author of ten books, family- and children-oriented. In 1994, she's writing a sequel to *Let's Make A Memory* (with Shirley Dobson), which sold half a million copies. The new one is titled *Let's Hide the Word,* dealing with "family fun things to do to teach Scripture."

Mrs. Gaither also teaches a songwriting class at Anderson University. "It's sort of funny," she said, "because, like Fanny Crosby, I've never written a single line of music. But what I basically say to the kids is that great songwriting comes from great lyrics. I tell them to read Frost and Sandburg and Wordsworth. The great old hymns don't live because they're old, they live because they're good. And the great hymns and great poems don't waste a single word. Not a word is there unless it has to be. . . . You can only call it a song if you've worked on the lyrics, worked on the music, and created something that can survive the style—something that can be rearranged in a new style."

Given his role in Christian music over more than thirty years, Bill was asked to give his assessment of that music as the twenty-first century approaches.

"I disagree," he said, "with the people who think that Christian music is going to be the next country music on the basis of mass popularity. The first time I was asked a question about that was in 1963. I said then I didn't think so. And in 1973 they asked me again—that kind of question seems to pop up every decade or so—and the answer was the same. Basically, you know, music is entertainment, it's diversion. And gospel music, when you get to the nuts and bolts of the Gospel, sooner or later we'll say, 'Now I would like to have your serious attention.' And I just don't think the masses are after something that's going to say 'I want your serious attention.'

"But I think that some of the best musical talent has always been in the church. I would put our talent—our singers and our players and our songwriters—on a par with anybody in the secular music field today. I feel very strongly about that. However, the lyrics, the *true* gospel lyrics, are probably always going to limit comparison with country music and other genres. Because we are showcasing a theology. That's what it's all about!''

9

Larnelle Harris

IT WAS NOT SOMETHING THAT LARNELLE HARRIS COULD have conceived of—even in his wildest imagining—when he was growing up in Danville, a one-time trading center in the "blue grass" region of Kentucky and one of the earliest settlements on the storied Wilderness Road as the country was expanding westward. That he would somehow be an eyewitness to substantial world history could not have been a very realistic appraisal of what would happen to a black youngster from Danville, Kentucky.

Yet, in what was akin to Shakespearean drama as the last decade of the twentieth century began, the entire fabric of a huge communist regime was being rent. The once seemingly impregnable Soviet bloc of Eastern Europe had already collapsed and, in three days of August 1991, there was a coup against the government of Soviet President Mikhail Gorbachev. Those three explosive days would bring an end to the power of the Communist Party, a flying apart of the Soviet Union itself, and a collapse of what was still left of the concepts of Marxism-Leninism.

Into that charged atmosphere, just a week after the coup, came the *Moscow Project* of the International Bible Society and Youth for Christ International, bringing with them the talents of gospel singer Larnelle Harris. He and his associates were to perform inside the Kremlin, the architectural symbol of former communist power, talking and singing to a large audience of Russians about God and freedom.

"It was one of the most exciting things I've ever been part of," Harris recalls, "because the Kremlin never had a role over the entire history of communism in what I believe is the most important thing in the world: the Gospel of Jesus Christ. And there I was in a hall with some 65-hundred people, talking to them and sharing songs about freedom—and one song in particular, 'Let Freedom Ring,' written by my good friends, Bill and Gloria Gaither.

"And I'm singing this and the people are responding and they're clapping their hands. So, with absolutely no political agenda whatsoever, I have this audience which is particularly interested in this word 'freedom.' And I'm telling them about a freedom that coups cannot affect, that no one can take away, that no one can steal—it's the freedom of the Lord Jesus Christ. And they're excited about it!"

While he was in Russia, Larnelle was part of a team to distribute, free of charge, four million copies of the Bible, translated into Russian. The Bible were as seeds scattered on the troubled soil of Russia; the gospel music was the sweet rain to nourish the seeds.

The harvest is yet to come.

Larnelle Harris was born in 1947, the youngest of six children (four sons, two daughters) of Oscar Jr. and Ida Mae Harris. His father was a baker by trade. Both of his parents sang in church; his father sang in the choir and with local quartets.

"I had a wonderful childhood," Larnelle said, "although it was very strict. My mom and dad were of the old school of discipline. We didn't have a lot in terms of monetary things, but my parents made certain that all of us had everything we needed. And, most of all, we knew that we had them."

There weren't a lot of travelling gospel groups coming through Danville when Larnelle was a youngster, "but I remember watching one of my favorites, who is still one of my favorites, Ray Charles on TV. And then I'd go and sit at the piano and rock back and forth and try to sing—that's a thing I remember."

His interest in music was really developed in grade school and nourished until he went to Western Kentucky University in Bowling Green to pursue a Bachelor of Arts in music education. While in college, he was part of a group called Gemini Fifteen—eleven women and four men, most of them music majors. They played "pop" music, mostly big band arrangements, and were in demand for USO shows in the Caribbean and Germany. Larnelle was the drummer in the band. But he also sang, most especially a solo of "Georgia," Ray Charles's big hit.

On graduation from Western Kentucky he joined a unique performance group called The Spurrlows. The concept of producer Thurlow Spurr, the group wasn't really in the gospel genre; more properly it could be described as an inspirational ensemble. Its recorded work ranged from "My Favorite Things" (Rodgers-Hammerstein) to "Bridge Over Troubled Water" (Simon) to "A Wonderful Day Like Today" (Bricusse-Newley) to an old folk melody like "Scarborough Fair." Again, Larnelle was the drummer who also sang some.

But the Spurrlows toured widely and during his more than two years with the group, Harris saw new doors opened to him. Word Records signed him, recognizing that the songs Larnelle was writing were just as important as his vocal performance. His first album at Word was titled "Tell It to Jesus," establishing him as a serious gospel artist. That was in 1975 and if there was any doubt about where Larnelle Harris was going in the field, it was dispelled by Word's assignment of veteran arranger-producer Bergen White to that album.

After three albums with Word, he moved to Impact Records in 1981, where his initial album, "Give Me More Love In My Heart," not only included five of his own songs but clearly established him as a gospel star. That album won the 1981 Dove Award as the contemporary black gospel album of the year. It was a time in his life where it was critically important for Larnelle Harris to have his head on straight.

That was really not a problem for him. He had long since ordered his priorities. They started with his faith, which led directly to his wife, Cynthia (called "Mitzy"), and his two young children, Lonnie and Teresa. He had met Mitzy at Western Kentucky University and, when they married, it was clear that she was to have her own career.

"Mitzy is a teacher in special education," Larnelle says proudly, "and I spend time giving her support, because the kids nowadays are so tough and so hard that what she does is quite a challenge. Not only does she help me but I help her, as well."

When his children were growing up, Larnelle's appointments were regulated by the school bus schedule. "I wanted to be there when they got home," he explained. "I couldn't always, but I tried. Kids are exposed to so much out in the world, and we want to keep the lines open with our kids to talk about things.

"That's why I'm thankful that we live so close to our parents. Lonnie's grandfather can teach him things that I'll never be able to. And watching my father-in-law interact with him, and renew his own youth, brings the song 'I Can Begin Again' to life in front of my eyes."

Today Lonnie is nineteen and a student at the University of Louisville on an academic scholarship. "My son, at this point," Larnelle said, "is a sax player and a music major. They have a very good jazz program at the university and Lonnie is heavily involved in that. He played on one of my albums, on a song about family called "Take the Time.' He did a great job."

Daughter Teresa is fourteen, in her first year of high school, and Larnelle reports she's a "basketball player and would-be scientist." She also sings some in church, helps with the children's choir, and has sung a duet or two with her father at the services.

The Maple Grove Baptist Church in Louisville is part of Harris's extended family. He has been a deacon and he does sing in church occasionally. "But I have more important things to do there," Larnelle said. "I'm chairman of the finance committee. I sing some but, thankfully, my pastor understands that I'm out giving all the time and sometimes I just need to sit. So I come in and sit with my family and take in the service."

He went on: "When I do a concert, I know there are as many different needs as there are people. Being involved in my local church has increased my sensitivity to people that I meet. I see my role as a performer as encouraging the flock, and it's important to share what the Lord is doing in my life now, not just last week or last month."

By 1983 the Dove Award voters had named him "Male Vocalist of the Year." He would be so honored again in 1986 and 1988. Larnelle's stint with the prestigious Gaither Vocal Band certainly moved his career forward. But it might be argued that his duet performances with Sandi Patti, the truly dominant female vocalist in the gospel field in the 1980s and early 1990s, took Larnelle Harris to another level of accomplishment.

In 1984, their duet of "I've Just Seen Jesus" won the Grammy Award as the best gospel performance by a duo or group. Just two years later Patti and Harris won the same award again for their rendition of "More Than Wonderful." Both recordings soared to the number-one spot on the Christian music charts.

Sandi Patti, whose marvelous voice has a three-octave range, won the Dove Award of the Gospel Music Association as female vocalist of the year for eleven consecutive years—from 1982 through 1992. She was the Dove Awards artist of the year (the top GMA individual honor) in 1982, 1984, 1985, 1987, and 1988. There seemed to be no end to it. She would win no less than sixteen *other* Dove Awards for albums of the year, for children's music albums of the year, for songs of the year (as a writer), and even for short-form video.

In the vernacular, Sandi "had it made."

Music journalist Don Cusic, writing in *BMI Magazine,* said of her: "Sandi Patti says that sometimes she'd rather be just a wife and mother with children pulling on her skirts while she's fixing dinner for her husband. But that's not the way God has planned it."

Cusic also wrote of her marriage to John Heverling, an accounting student she met while studying music at Anderson, Indiana, College, reporting that John "takes care of all Sandi's bookings, travel arrangements and bookkeeping, as well as running the sounds and lights of her concerts. 'John is part of everything I do and everything that I am,' said Sandi. 'He's in control of everything.' ''

Then, suddenly (or so it seemed to outsiders) Sandi's idyllic world came tumbling down. There was the destruction by arson of her Anderson, Indiana, office headquarters, the painful ending of her marriage and the subsequent hateful publicity, and the slow, equally painful, process of uncovering her childhood sexual abuse at the hands of a family acquaintance. The toll was terrible.

''I looked like I had it all together,'' Sandi admitted. ''Not that what I've shared in the past hasn't been me . . . but I've unintentionally given some sort of fairytale portrayal of my life.''

The healing process began when she returned to the recording studio for work on the Word/Epic album, *Le Voyage,* a concept for a story album dealing with a traveller's voyage through life brought to Sandi by producer Greg Nelson and Christian music veteran Bob Farrell:

With the wind at my back . . . the journey before me
I set my feet on the road that leads to life
And take the hand of the One who'll be my companion
For He will show me the place to begin.

''This album has really become a journey for me,'' Sandi said. ''It's been a wonderful place to put my questions and my doubts, my joys and sorrows and ups and downs. I *had* to do this project . . . I was *compelled* to do it. The story of the Traveller is my story; it's our story. I have sung for so many years about experiencing victory in Jesus, and the music I share will continue to do so. I just want to add—there is joy in the process as well, when we walk with the Lord, our Companion.''

The healing process for Sandi was also helped along

when she toured with fellow artists and friends on the popular Young Messiah Tour—an annual tour of multiple gospel artists conducted "in the round" in major cities between Thanksgiving and Christmas.

And while the personnel changes from time to time, Larnelle Harris has been on the tour every year it has been produced. Sandi Patti is also a regular on the Young Messiah Tour.

"When there are off days on the tour," Larnelle said, "I go home. I save my frequent flier miles and head for the airport. And Sandi did too. And so we were often on the same plane with the same destination— heading home."

Even though he plays a hundred-plus performance dates a year he is never comfortable with the touring. "Since I'm not a great traveller, it's pretty rough. I enjoy what I do when I get there, but as soon as I'm done I want to come home."

The creative process—the songwriting—is different with almost every person. With Larnelle it is hard work. "Guys talk about inspiration in this process," he said. " 'I wrote this from inspiration, or that from inspiration.' And I guess some people do that. But for me it's simply sitting down, having an idea and saying 'This idea must say this. I'm not going to let it wander. It must say what I intend.' And with the computer—the one that's in my head—I start sifting through all the wonderful words we have in our language and try to find just the right words. And that's work.

"With me, you might say that inspiration comes in terms of the idea; the inspiration coming from the work of reading and studying things around me and dissecting life around me. Then that idea turns to work when it comes to putting lyrics on a piece of paper, taking the idea and making it live. And it's work again when I try to get a vocal melody and music to surround the idea. And it becomes work yet again when you record it and try to make it something that touches the heart and moves the soul.''

Why is it then that all great songs seem to be so simple?

''Because somebody did the *work* of really thinking them through.'' The answer was firm and certain.

Larnelle's hard work has clearly paid off. He was honored with the Dove Award as songwriter of the year in 1988, just a year after his performance of ''How Excellent Is Thy Name,'' written by Dick and Melodie Tunney, contributed to making it the Dove Award song of the year. The recording of ''How Excellent Is Thy Name'' also won for Larnelle the Grammy Award for the best solo gospel performance of 1986.

In 1988 there was another Grammy Award for ''best gospel performance, male'' for the album *The Father Hath Provided,* the title song of which was written by Larnelle and had soared to the number-one position on the Christian music charts. Again in 1989 he won the same Grammy for his album, *Larnelle . . . Christmas.*

His hard work, his faith, and his talent shines through everything he does and it is not an exaggeration to say that his songwriting seems to get better with every succeeding album.

In his 1988 album, *I Can Begin Again,* the title cut (co-written with Dave Clark) is an upbeat, rhythmic tune with present-day connotations. It carefully sets the premise of its story in the first verse:

> *Alone again in a crowded room*
> *Cornered by the questions in my mind*
> *It's so hard to understand,*
> *How the life that I had planned*
> *Stole my joy and left me far behind.*

But hope is injected into the story when Larnelle sings: ''I can look beyond the skies, deep into the Father's eyes/ And see that there is hope for one like me'':

> *I can begin again*
> *With the passion of a child*
> *My heart has caught a vision*
> *Of a life that's still worthwhile.*
> *I can reach out again*
> *Far beyond what I have done*
> *Like a dreamer who's awakened*
> *To a life that's yet to come*
> *For new beginnings are not just for the young.*

The great hope offered listeners took ''I Can Begin Again'' to the number-one spot on Christian music charts.

His 1992 album, *I Choose Joy,* was the underpinning of his successful 1993 tour in troubled South Africa. The words of the theme song of the tour offered reality *and* hope:

> *To tell the truth this world is full of trouble*
> *And if we live long enough it's sure to come our way*
> *We've a choice to walk in fear and trembling*
> *Or claim the victory that's already ours this very day*

> *I choose joy*
> *I'll never let the problems keep me down*
> *'Cause the Lord is working all things out for my good*
> *I choose joy.*

Larnelle has had fifteen albums released since 1975. The latest, *Beyond All Limits* (1994), is further affirmation of his solid faith. The album includes a reprise of Oliver Holden's traditional anthem, ''All Hail the

Power (Of Jesus's Name).'' Harris's powerful tenor soars on this one.

The Kentuckian's career has expressions over a broad spectrum. He is the national spokesperson for the International Bible Society, for World Vision, and for the Zondervan Family Bookstores. He was the featured vocalist on the title cut for the movie, *Born Again,* based on the life of Watergate principal Chuck Colson.

And then there is Larnelle's recording of Jerome Olds's ''Mighty Spirit,'' featured on the nationally televised public service announcements for the Points of Light Foundation, growing out of President George Bush's call for renewed public service volunteerism in the nation. Harris's *a cappella* rendition is truly exciting.

He was also the co-writer of ''Castle of Hope,'' the theme song for GlenCastle, a low-income housing development in Atlanta, one of President Bush's ''points of light.''

Involved in life: that's Larnelle Harris.

10

Steven Curtis Chapman

THERE IS NO SUCH THINGS AS GENUINE OVERNIGHT stardom in show business. But if there were, then Steven Curtis Chapman, a handsome, baby-faced product of Kentucky, would likely be first in line to qualify. It's a question of perception.

For as the decade of the eighties was winding down, he just seemed to burst full-blown onto the gospel music scene: an assured performer on stage, a talented songwriter, fully accepted by an adoring following of fans, honored with the most prestigious awards in the music world, complete with a picture-perfect mid-America family. And level-headed about it all.

In mid-1992, after he had twice been named Gospel Artist of the Year, he told an interviewer: "It's tough when people perceive what they see as an 'overnight success,' though to some degree there is a measure of reality in that concept for me. But I started writing songs ten years ago, coming to Nashville from Paducah, having songs torn apart by publishers, and leaving in tears at times. But now I sit out here [in the rural outskirts of Nashville] and am overwhelmed that I get to do something I enjoy.''

That enjoyment of music came to him shortly after he was born in Paducah, Kentucky, thirty-two years ago, for his father was the proprietor of a music store and a writer of country songs. ''I can remember,'' Chapman said, ''how my dad used to close the kitchen door and he and his buddies would write country music all hours of the night. I remember thinking it was a kind of a mystery, shrouded in secrecy, and I always wondered what was going on in there. I guess it was only natural I try my hand at songwriting.''

Natural indeed. At the age of six he was playing a guitar, by eight he had made a commitment as a Christian, and he was a sophomore in high school when he wrote his first song.

''My first song was a gospel song I wrote while riding on the tractor one day,'' he recalled. ''I remember stopping the tractor, running up to the house, getting a piece of paper and starting to write those words down. I played guitar, bass, and drums [by that time] and had always toyed with writing songs. But as far as really writing my first song and feeling like I had come up with something creative and fresh, that was it. That got the wheels in motion.''

At that time he was being influenced by artists who were pushing the religious music envelope, trending away from the traditional Southern gospel sounds. Included in this number were Dallas Holm, the Archers, the exciting Imperials quartet, Andrae Crouch, and one Harvey Jett, late of the Black Oak Arkansas band, who was playing churches and impressing young Chapman with his ''relaxed, conversational way on stage that really communicated with the people. I also saw how humor would set people at ease, and how they would maybe believe you a little more when you become vulnerable.''

Still, Steven was not quite sure he would opt for a musical career. He briefly flirted with pre-med classes at Anderson, Indiana, College—an institution which has spawned a number of gospel artists—before making his final decision. It was to be music; Nashville, ''Music City U. S. A.,'' was the lure.

While in college, then, he worked summers in the shows in the big Opryland amusement park in Nashville (as did his brother, Herb), singing and dancing. ''I can clog with the best of them,'' he says, laughing.

Like the Hollywood of old, Nashville can be a place in which show business lightning can strike. And so it was with Steven Curtis Chapman. The printed programs for the Opryland shows carried small blurbs about the young entertainers. Steven's said that he was a songwriter who wrote gospel tunes. Enter Danny Daniels, who had read the little bio. He approached Chapman after a show the Opryland troupe was doing in Gatlinburg to promote the Nashville amusement park.

Steven remembers vividly what happened then. ''There was door #1 [opening] that I didn't even have to knock on. This guy came up to me and said 'play me your songs.' And he seemed to like what he heard. . . . Then he called me one night [at college] and said, 'I played some of your songs for one of my friends tonight. She's been doing a little bit of traveling with Bill Gaither. I went to school with her and she's interested in recording one song in particular on her next album. She's done one album and it's starting to go well. We believe she's going to do really well. She's really going to be a powerhouse in gospel music somewhere down the line.' ''

Daniels told him the woman's name was Sandi Patti.

Steven had never heard of her and he confesses now that he was very naive about the music business at the time.

"Maybe we should hang onto those songs," he told Daniels, "and pitch them to the Imperials and more established artists. What do you think? Am I being totally dumb?"

Daniels didn't answer him directly. "Well," he said, "it won't hurt to pitch them around a bit."

But the offer from this Sandi Patti nagged at him. He began to check around the Nashville music fraternity about her. Yes, he was told, Sandi Patti is certainly slated for future stardom. By the time he changed his mind, however, Patti had made her choices for her second album, and Chapman's song was *not* included. He had learned an important lesson.

(Since that time, she has cut several Chapman songs, including "Love Will Be Our Home," which garnered a Dove Award nomination for best inspirational recorded song.)

Chapman came to understand after the abortive Patti episode that interrelationships within the gospel music family were vital to him. "You can knock on doors yourself," he has said, "but when someone like Bill Gaither walks in and says, 'this is really good and you need to listen to this kid,' people take note. And I had people like that helping me along the way."

Once the doors are open, however, talent must take over. And as a songwriter Steven clearly had the talent. Sandi Patti also cut his "Give Him the Glory," White Heart recorded "Carried Away," the Cathedrals released his "I Can See the Hand," and country megastar Glen Campbell included Steven's "A Day In America" in an album tribute to the Statue of Liberty. Most recently he co-wrote "The Business of Love" with southern country rock leader Charlie Daniels for Daniels's highly touted first gospel album, "The Door" (*see* Chapter 12).

In 1986, Chapman signed with Sparrow Records. Now he wasn't only a songwriter but, thanks to his experience with the Opryland shows, he was also a polished performer.

In the following year, his first CD album, titled *First Hand,* produced by Phil Naish, was released to strong reviews. The album was nominated for a GMA Dove Award as contemporary album of the year and one of the tunes on that album, "Hiding Place," got the Dove nomination for song of the year. Suddenly, it seemed, Steven Curtis Chapman was *the* hot name in contemporary gospel music. "First Hand" was among the top fifty albums of 1987, with three songs from the album—"Weak Days," "Hiding Place," and "Run Away"—vaulting into top-five positions on the gospel charts. Trade journals were calling him the best new artist of the year.

By that time, Steven was a married man. He had met his wife-to-be at Anderson College in Indiana, a meeting that came about because they had identical last names.

His wife, Mary Beth, explained: "We shared a mailbox at college because our last names were the same. And so we basically ended up going out on a date just because our last names were the same. It was a situation of 'Hah, hah, wouldn't it be funny if we got married.' "

On October 13, 1984, they did marry, with Mary Beth Chapman Chapman, who liked to think of herself as a very organized, structured person, inheriting a whirlwind, so to speak. As Steven's career took off like a rocket, Mary Beth had to try to adjust to a hectic lifestyle she really hadn't anticipated.

"I was actually keeping my eyes open for a steady

nine-to-five type,'' she said. ''I had to deal with that early in our marriage because nothing seemed organized at all.'' Mary Beth laughed heartily. ''You never knew what was going to happen next! I guess it's just learning what's normal for our family. That doesn't mean that I don't get frustrated. When he's on tour, that's the hardest season of the year because of the children not getting to see him as much. It's definitely difficult.''

(Today the Chapmans have three towheaded children: Emily, age eight; Caleb, four; and Will Franklin, three.)

Steven was not unfeeling about the stresses his career had placed on his wife. At one point, feeling somewhat guilty about it, he turned to his father-in-law for advice. He recalls: ''My wife's father worked thirty years in an International Harvester plant, and I told him once that I felt like I should just get a regular job in a factory and provide a stable income for my family like he did. He interrupted me and said, 'If you ever do that, I'll turn around and beat ya,' because even though he's had a good life, he's had some regrets for not following *his* dreams.''

Perhaps Chapman's own dreams reached a culmination—certainly a high point—on an April night in 1993 when, in the Tennessee Performing Arts Center, he won no less than six Dove Awards given by the members of the Gospel Music Association, including three top honors as artist of the year, male vocalist of the year, and songwriter of the year. He called Mary Beth up from the audience to stand by his side: two glowing young people, each proud of the other.

In his CD album that year, the best-selling *The Great Adventure,* Steven included an unabashed love song to Mary Beth, ''Go There With You'':

*I will take a heart whose nature is to beat for
   me alone,*

*And fill it up with you, make all your joy and
    pain my own.
No matter how deep a valley you go through,
I will go there with you.*

Sparrow Records, recognizing the broad appeal of
the song, released it as a single not only to the Christian
market but to country and pop radio stations as well.
It reached number one on the charts, as did the album
itself and two other singles from the CD: "Where We
Belong" and the title cut, "The Great Adventure."

Clearly this album, only his fifth to that point, was
what the record industry calls a "breakout." It was
recorded live at a sold-out concert date in Seattle,
Washington, and was an innovation in contemporary
Christian music, containing elements of rock, rap, and
a quiet, contemplative acoustical medley of five songs
with a distinct country "feel," even though the message was a Christian one. In many different ways, then,
Chapman was telling his young audiences that "The
Great Adventure" was one with God:

*Saddle up your horses, we've got a trail to blaze
Through the wild blue yonder of God's amazing
    grace.
Let's follow our leader into the glorious
    unknown,
This is a life like no other,
This is the Great Adventure!*

The release of the love song, "Go There With You,"
to country and pop radio stations revived speculation
that has hounded Steven ever since his own great adventure as a performer began. Would he, given the fiscal realities of the business, become the latest gospel
music star to stage a crossover to country music? It can

be guessed that there are some in Nashville trying to advise him to go that route. The question has been asked of him more than once by knowledgeable writers in the music field.

Deborah Evans Price asked it early, in an interview for *American Songwriter* in the summer of 1989. "I made it a goal of mine real early not to get locked into any one style," Chapman replied. "However, being known as a gospel songwriter makes it hard to get secular cuts. It's tough. When we send a song to a producer they perceive it differently. It's just like if we received a song from a secular publisher, whether you want to or not there's just the reality that you catch yourself looking at it differently, but we give it a listen. In the back of some people's minds they think the writer doesn't understand this genre or style. What it means to me is that I've got to write a song that is head and shoulders above all the other writers that are right there with the pulse of what's going in country or pop music."

Ms. Price added: "Chapman readily acknowledges that he wants to have tunes recorded in the secular field, but says he won't compromise his values. The songs won't be overtly religious, but he couldn't write anything that contradicted his beliefs."

In the July 1992 issue of *CCM* (*Christian Contemporary Music*) magazine, senior editor Thom Granger brought up the subject again. The answer—two years after the *American Songwriter* interview—was more expansive.

Chapman said: "I've had a chance this year to write with about six guys that are successful country writers, and it's been a way for me to stretch beyond my comfort zone—beyond all the people that I normally surround myself with, who talk the same language, so to speak. It's been a great way to forge new relationships;

professionally first, but a lot of these guys have a real faith in God.

"Every one of them has a desire to write great songs—not by formula and not writing with specific artists in mind—none of those things ever came up, which surprised me, because it does in Christian music. And these guys wanted to work with me because they wanted to write songs with hope; songs that would have a positive effect on people. Guys like Paul Overstreet have had a tremendous impact in the music business as well as with the listeners. He gets mail from people who respond to the ideas in his songs, and then he'll write back to them and say, 'The reason I wrote that was because . . .' and really witness the love of God to them one-on-one.

"As far as making an all-country album, I'll tell you . . . I've developed these relationships with country artists and writers [and have] had the president of a country label ask if I ever considered crossing over into country, and I'm not even knocking on doors! . . .

"I don't really understand it, but at this point I feel like I'd be contriving something—which is something I swore myself against—to not do this music that is coming out of me most naturally. At the same time, I think I've been led into these writing relationships where that avenue can be creatively explored."

A thoroughly logical conclusion can be that even though Steven Curtis Chapman may not be knocking on country music doors they are not locked to him. They may even be ajar.

As this book was being completed in the spring of 1994, the sixth Chapman CD album, *Heaven and the Real World,* was being readied for release. It was designed to give encouragement to listeners to live the spiritual life in a tough world. Coincident with the release of the album was the publication of Steven's first book, *Finding Heaven in the Real World,* a thirty-day devotional book that deals with such topics as understanding the love and grace of God, escaping temptations, and replacing ''wishful thinking'' with real faith and conviction.

He debuted the title cut of the new album on the April 1994 Dove Awards telecast, making clear that ''Jesus is heaven in the real world.''

In the awards ceremonies Chapman was named the gospel songwriter of the year for the sixth consecutive time. Also the love song for his wife, ''Go There With You,'' was declared to be the Contemporary Recorded Song of the Year. Add to that a Dove Award for his long-form video of ''The Great Adventure'' concert, and his cache of Doves had reached nineteen.

Three times the gospel artist of the year, three times the gospel male vocalist of the year, and the winner of three Grammy Awards for gospel albums, Steven remains on top of the gospel music field.

11

❧

Twila Paris

"*I*NEVITABLE" IS DEFINED AS THAT WHICH "CANNOT be avoided, evaded, or escaped; sure to befall, happen, or come, by the very nature of things (as, one's *inevitable* fate)."

That word also defines the young life of Twila Paris, for it seems certain there was no way she could have avoided being what she has become: one of the most respected writers of prayerful ballads and one of the most popular gospel singers on the contemporary scene. She was literally born to it.

"My great-grandfather was a minister," Twila explains. "My grandmother was the oldest of four sisters; there were four sisters and a brother. And the family travelled together in a covered wagon all over Arkansas and Oklahoma and would build brush arbors and they'd have meetings. They'd go wherever the Lord was telling them to go and stay however long they felt like He said stay and usually a church would be born. Then they'd move on to another place just like Christian gypsies, this travelling band of ministers.

143

"My grandma used to write songs and they'd make copies and to help support the ministry they'd sell them for a nickle on the street. . . . I really do exactly what they did, exactly what my grandmother was doing some seventy years ago. I don't know if it's in the genes or a family calling."

Genes? Family calling? However it might be described, Twila Inez Paris, now in her mid-thirties, is a product of inevitable fate.

The daughter of Oren and Inez Paris, she was born in Fort Worth, Texas, the first child of four. But she was raised in the small community of Springdale, Arkansas, where her father had gone to take a role in a ministry called "Youth With A Mission," founded by Twila's uncle, Loren Cunningham.

Oren was himself a gospel songwriter and encouraged his precocious daughter who "made up songs and ran around the house singing them" when she was only two. By the age of five she was taking piano lessons. "My grandmother started me," Twila recalls, "and she didn't just give me a lesson once a week. She stood over me every day for an hour and watched me practice!"

Twila started to write songs when she was twelve "because my Dad assigned me—he was my piano teacher then—to write a song. He had been teaching me about music theory and improvisation and had assigned me to write a song—and I said, 'I can't.' "

But in the warm cocoon of family, she soon found that she *could* write songs. There was music all around her: she played the flute in her junior high school band and sang in her high school chorus and in a special ensemble called "Unity." And the songwriting continued.

"I wrote bad songs for several years," she confessed.

"At first I didn't think seriously about being a song-writer. It was just a creative outlet. Then, when I was seventeen [and a senior in high school], I wrote a song or two that I thought could be real songs."

With that impetus the next step, as a potential professional singer-songwriter, presented itself. She and her father approached a friend who ran a small Christian record company in Kansas for advice. He suggested that they record a custom album—meaning a self-financed recording—to get the attention of major record labels. And the Parises did that, taking a bank loan to finance the effort. (It is part of the lore of the Twila Paris story that it took some four years before she could make enough money as a professional to repay the bank loan.)

In any event, the advice they received in Kansas City paid dividends. Record producer Wayne Boosahda heard the custom album and brought Twila to the attention of executives at Milk and Honey Records, a company noted for giving starts to young potential Christian artists. They signed her and, in 1981, released her first album: *Knowin' You're Around,* produced by Boosahda and Ken Sarkey. All of the songs on that album were written by Twila—it has been the hallmark of her work ever since.

In 1982, Milk and Honey released a second album, *Keeping My Eyes On You;* the third, in 1984, was titled *The Warrior Is A Child.* Clearly, she had become a gospel music talent to be reckoned with; so much so that Milk and Honey released an album in 1985 offering *The Best of Twila Paris.*

A demand grew for her appearance on the concert circuit. At the age of twenty-one she needed someone to handle her bookings. Dad Oren gave the job to a young associate at the Youth With A Mission headquarters, one Jack Wright.

Wright had come to Fayetteville, Arkansas, to attend the University of Arkansas; the Paris family then lived near the university. "While in college," Twila recalled, "Jack became a Christian and heard about Youth With A Mission and joined the staff with my father. And Jack would book me to sing somewhere, and I'd represent YWAM and give my testimony through music."

In storybooks, a whirlwind romance between Twila Paris and Jack Wright would ensue. But that's not the way it was. She had known him since she was seventeen; he had joined the YWAM ministry when Twila was a senior in high school. And it was in high school that she came under the influence of a youth leader who offered her guidance about dating.

"At first I thought she was from the Dark Ages," Twila said. "She told me that her husband was the first man she'd ever kissed. I couldn't believe it. I thought that was really stupid. But you know what? That somehow found a way into my head and helped me set some high dating standards for myself. I was friends with everyone, but I was extremely selective with whom I dated."

So, although Twila and Jack were closely allied in her career, seven years would go by before they actually began dating. And she knew him for nine years before they married.

"And you know what?" she told interviewer Susie Shellenberger, "I treasure that fact that my husband is the only man I've ever given any of myself to physically. This is the only man I've ever been with. And I'm the only woman he's ever been with. Do you understand the security in that? There's never any weird comparisons going on here. I have absolutely no reason to get jealous or feel threatened. I can be totally vulnerable and completely secure, and he can, too. That's the way God intended marriage to be—to *embrace* us, not threaten us."

The craft of songwriter is a major concern for Twila. She is not prolific; the writing comes in spurts. "I may write several songs in one week, and then may not write again for several months. . . . I hope that after seventeen years of songwriting I have developed my craft and gotten more skilled at the art, which I believe it is to a degree. And yet at the core I still tend to start the song on a very visceral level. . . . I believe sometimes the songs that are felt the deepest are the ones that start at that level. . . .

"Not everybody likes the songs that I write, but the people who do often tell me I've written exactly what they are feeling. So I feel my songs are garments that other people can take and put on and make their own. A lot of songs are written directly like a prayer. People can take that song and it becomes their song and their prayer. Obviously I don't have the market cornered on this, but I feel that what makes a song special is when listeners can take it and make it theirs."

Twila has been called a "modern-day hymnwriter" and has been compared favorably with the legendary Fanny Crosby for her contributions to hymnody—which is quite a plaudit for one so young. It's a fact, however, that such Paris compositions as "We Will Glorify," "Lamb of God," "How Beautiful," "Faithful Men," and "He Is Exalted" are included in church hymnals around the world. It ought to be pointed out, also, that Aunt Fanny was basically a lyricist; the young lady from Arkansas has always done it all—words and music.

Music journalist Deborah Evans Price, who knows songwriters (gospel and country) better than most, pointed out that the Paris career as a songwriter is un-

usual because she has never pitched her songs to anyone else and she has rarely been a collaborator.
"Because Twila is not prolific," Price wrote, "she usually has just enough songs to record her own albums.
That hasn't stopped her songs from being recorded by
others. Numerous acts have covered her songs and
they've been translated into many different languages."

But . . . *after* Twila has introduced them.

That circumstance has given her albums a "new-
ness" rarely seen in the gospel genre. Everything
doesn't *seem* new, it *is* new. The message is a familiar
one, of course, but Paris's songs experiment with different ways to handle the words and with new sounds
through which to transmit the message.

There are several examples of that in her album *Beyond A Dream* (Star Song, 1993). For instance, this is
the entire lyric package for one of the cuts:

> *Oh, the light is shining*
> *I can feel it warm and glowing*
> *Oh, the day is breaking*
> *Waking here inside my longing heart.*

The instrumentation is equally sparse: two organlike
keyboards and a piano. The mood is unhurried; slow
and tender. Twila's voice is even softer than usual;
there's an intimacy in how she sings here that is very
moving. Don't be surprised if some secular female vocalist picks it up and makes a "pop" hit of it. Whitney
Houston, who has solid gospel roots, comes to mind.

(This is the point, no doubt, to say that Twila Paris
is *not* a "belter" in a musical genre that thrives on
"belters," both male and female. But her voice is
strong and clear; the diction is precise—her lyrics are
never misunderstood.)

In the same album that offers the four-line song

quoted above, there is also a story song, more than twice the length in performance time than "The Light Is Shining," and telling the story of "Seventy years ago my father's mother's father/Led the clan of Nicholson," those brush arbor evangelists who were Twila's ancestors.

Twila wrote it for her grandmother's ninetieth birthday anniversary, acknowledging the debt she owed to those who had gone before her:

Sometimes I feel like a pale reflection
Living in the blessing they passed down
Some of them have held me
Some never knew my name
But the secret has been found
I want to give this to my children
And when I am very old
I hope there still will be a story worth the telling
Of seventy years ago.

Beyond A Dream, which shot to the top of the charts in music trade magazines, was Twila's first completely new album in more than two years. She had taken a total sabbatical from recording and touring in 1992, explaining that the "decision was the result of one of those times where I really did sense the Lord telling me what to do. We had been doing a lot of heavy touring, on the road two-and-a-half to three weeks a month for far too long. In addition to that, Jack's health has experienced a setback, and he was under tremendous physical and emotional stress."

Her husband has suffered from Epstein-Barr disease, more commonly known as chronic fatigue syndrome, for a number of years. So, together, they went through a healing process in the comfortable confines of their familiar Arkansas landscape.

"So part of what has been so wonderful for us," Twila told *CCM* senior editor Thom Granger when the sabbatical was ended, "has been to back off and rest and spend time together with the Lord. We've even received some counseling, to better help us understand some of these problems, and how they affect every part of our being. For us it's been like the verse in Psalm Twenty-three that states, 'He leads me beside the still waters/He restores my soul.' "

Given the unrelenting competition of the recording business, the executive of Star Song records covered the period of the sabbatical by releasing an album—titled *A Heart That Knows You*—which was basically a collection of twelve Paris familiar favorites, marking the tenth year of her professional career. One reviewer called it a "treasure," another said the album was "one of the best of the best."

Then in April of 1993, the sabbatical ended and work begun on the *Beyond A Dream* album, Twila received the Gospel Music Association's Dove Award as female vocalist of the year. That ended the consecutive eleven-year reign of gospel superstar Sandi Patti. It's interesting to note that another substantial female star, Amy Grant, had never won the female vocalist of the year Dove even though she had four times been named the gospel artist of the year—in 1983, 1986, 1989, and 1992.

Further recognition of Twila Paris's rise to the top of the gospel music field was her selection as the official spokesperson for The Parable Group, a marketing association of some three hundred independent Christian bookstores.

She told a news conference called to announce her association with The Parable Group: "The enemy is out there, and he's aggressive. Now is the time for faithful men and women of God to share God's word in a powerful, overwhelming way.''

In April of 1994 a perky Twila Paris performed her song "God Is In Control," obviously once more in control herself as a performer. And her commercials for The Parable Group Christian bookstores were scattered throughout the awards telecast.

She won the Gospel Female Vocalist of the Year Dove for the second time.

The road ahead is clear, flooded by the sunshine of her exceptional talent.

12

❧

The Country Connection

HANK WILLIAMS WAS A MAN OF BRILLIANT LIGHT and dark shadows. Fortunately, it's the light that prevails today—light shining through the one hundred and thirty songs he wrote, light reflecting from his numerous gold records, light illuminating the impact of his personal appearances.

He lived only twenty-nine years; in only the last six of those years could he have been considered to be a nationally known figure. Nevertheless, probably no performer in the history of country music has had more impact than Hank Williams.

No one can deny that dark shadows prevailed in his short life. He was a consummate sinner, which is not a judgment but a reality. Yet, like so many of his substantial contemporaries in the country music genre, he was also a gospel singer and songwriter. He was born in the southern gospel tradition that flowed in the veins of so many prominent gospel artists.

His mother, Lilly, was a church organist, and young Hank sat on the bench beside her during many evangelistic services. In later years, although never a churchgoer, that upbringing manifested itself in the country gospel songs that peppered his comparatively small catalog, as well as in the moralistic recitations he recorded as "Luke the Drifter."

He wrote the likes of "Are You Walking and A-Talking for the Lord," "A Home in Heaven," "(Heavenly Father) Help Me Understand," "A House of Gold," "How Can You Refuse Him Now?," "I'm Going Home," "(When I Get to Glory) I'm Gonna Sing," "Jesus Died for Me," "Jesus Is Calling," "Last Night I Dreamed of Heaven," "Wealth Won't Save Your Soul," "When God Comes and Gathers His Jewels," "When the Book of Life is Read," "(Can't You Hear the Blessed Saviour) Calling You," and the gospel classic, "I Saw the Light," recorded over and over again by both country and gospel performers:

> *I wandered so aimless, life filled with sin*
> *I wouldn't let my dear Saviour in,*
> *Then Jesus came like a stranger in the night,*
> *Praise the Lord, I saw the light.*

> *I saw the light, I saw the light,*
> *No more darkness, no more night,*
> *Now I'm so happy, no sorrow in sight,*
> *Praise the Lord, I saw the light.*

But Williams's truly profligate life of booze and pills finally caught up with him. On January 1, 1953, Hank died in the backseat of his chauffeur-driven Cadillac on his way to an engagement at Canton, Ohio. Official cause of death was "alcoholic cardiomyopathy." Simply put, that was a fatal heart disease brought on by excessive drinking.

In Canton that night, a spotlight was played on an empty theater stage while Hank's recording of "I Saw the Light" blared over loudspeakers. The audience wept.

Several days later, Williams's funeral in Montgomery, Alabama, was a massive outpouring of grief. Twenty-five thousand people tried to crowd into a city auditorium that had seats for only twenty-seven hundred. Women fainted; men cried openly. One reporter wrote that the funeral was "the greatest emotional orgy in the city's history since the inauguration of Jefferson Davis" as president of the Confederate States of America. Grand Ole Opry star Ernest Tubb, standing beside a silver casket, sang "Beyond the Sunset," Roy Acuff reprised "I Saw the Light," and Red Foley, choking back tears, sang Thomas A. Dorsey's poignant "Peace in the Valley."

Posthumously, Hank's records, especially "I'll Never Get Out of This World Alive," dominated the country music charts throughout 1953. For a time the charts were so full of Hank Williams that several record companies complained to the music trade journals on behalf of their living artists, denied places on the charts by the continuing appeal of Williams.

Even today, the Hank Williams catalog remains one of the most lucrative in the music publishing business. It seems strange that some contemporary gospel artist doesn't dig into that treasure trove and record a new album of Hank's gospel songs. The great appeal is still there.

There was a time when no self-respecting country music act would tour without gospel songs in the repertoire, almost always used to cap the evening's performance. Indeed, one of the most dominant country stars of all time—Roy Claxton Acuff—built the start of his career on the strength of a unique, and puzzling, gospel song titled "The Great Speckled Bird."

When he was just starting in East Tennessee in the 1930s, Acuff heard "The Great Speckled Bird" performed by a singer named Charlie Swain. The lyrics had been written by one Reverend Guy Smith; the melody was a traditional English tune. Acuff liked the sound of it and paid Swain fifty cents to copy down the lyrics for him. It would become Acuff's song; he would sing it thousands of times during his long and colorful career.

By 1936, Acuff and his troupe—called the Crazy Tennesseans then—had achieved enough of a reputation to be asked to record for the big American Record Company.

"They wanted 'The Bird,' " Acuff said, "they didn't want me."

That modesty aside, Acuff and his musicians went to Chicago to record *twenty* songs in their first recording session, including, of course, "The Great Speckled Bird":

> *What a beautiful thought I am thinking*
> *Concerning a great speckled bird;*
> *Remember her name is recorded*
> *On the pages of God's Holy Word. . . .*
> *When He cometh descending from heaven*
> *On the clouds, as He writes in His words;*
> *I'll be joyfully carried to meet Him*
> *On the wings of that great speckled bird.*

It is said that the Reverend Mr. Smith used as his source the ninth verse of the twelfth chapter of the Book of Jeremiah in the Old Testament: "Mine heritage is unto me as a speckled bird, the birds round are against her; come ye, assemble all the beasts of the field, come to devour." The bird, then, was regarded as an allegorical symbol, picturing the church as a group of persecuted individuals destined to gain eternal salvation as a reward for their earthly travail.

But it cannot be said that Acuff paid a great deal of attention to such detail. When The New King James Version of the Bible was published in 1979 Biblical scholars, with a charge to "sensitively polish the archaisms and vocabulary of the 1611 [King James] version," felt it necessary to change the text to read: "My heritage is to Me like a speckled vulture; The vultures all around are against her. Come, assemble all the beasts of the field, Bring them to devour!"

In my own interviews with Roy while writing *Grand Ole Opry,* a history, I mentioned to him that the "speckled bird" had been changed to a "speckled vulture." He shrugged, then grinned: "Believe me, it'll always be the great speckled bird to me."

Perhaps it was the public domain English tune that led to the popularity of the song. After all, the tune was also used on the country classic, "I'm Thinking Tonight of My Blue Eyes" by the country music pioneers, The Carter Family. Later the same melody was used in Hank Thompson's country hit, "The Wild Side of Life," in which the storyline was that men were led down the primrose path by ladies of easy virtue, characterized as "honky-tonk angels." Almost immediately, songwriter J. D. Miller came up with an answer song—a *woman's* answer—written to the same tune and putting the blame on men. It made an instant star of singer Kitty Wells.

"The Great Speckled Bird" wasn't the only gospel song in Roy Acuff's career. Among his best known recordings were "Turn Your Radio On" and "I'll Fly

Away,'' both written by the prolific Albert E. Brumley, an Oklahoman who is regarded as one of the greatest gospel composers of all time.

Acuff also recorded the likes of ''That Glory Bound Train,'' which he wrote with Odell McLeod; ''Lord, Build Me A Cabin In Glory,'' ''Somebody Touched Me,'' ''Traveling the Highway Home,'' Acuff's own ''The Precious Jewel,'' ''The Family Who Prays (Never Shall Part),'' ''Radio Station S-A-V-E-D,'' ''Life's Railway To Heaven,'' and more.

Even Acuff's theme song, ''Wabash Cannonball,'' had lyrics adapted to the gospel, with the Wabash Cannonball train carrying passengers ''home to victory'' after ''the earthly race is over.''

When Roy Acuff came to the Grand Ole Opry in 1938, the star of that important country music radio show was clearly Uncle Dave Macon of Smart Station, Tennessee, a flamboyant, grinning, self-assured singer and banjo player, who billed himself as ''The World's Greatest Banjo Player.'' He, too, had been raised in the southern gospel tradition, even though many of his songs were secular ones.

While he played and sang all of his life in backroads Tennessee, he didn't become a professional entertainer until he was fifty years old. For years he had operated a successful freight-hauling business known as the Macon Midway Mules and Transportation Company. He operated between Woodbury, the county seat of Cannon County, and Murfreesboro, the county seat of Rutherford County. It was a two-day mule-and-wagon trip between those two points and his most profitable cargo was Jack Daniel's No. 7 whiskey, carried at a fee of twenty-five cents a gallon.

The advent of the internal combustion engine put him out of business, a development he could never forget or forgive. One of the songs he sang at the Grand Ole Opry, more or less gospel in orientation, said:

> *You can talk about your evangelists,*
> *You can talk about Mister Ford, too;*
> *But Henry is a-shaking more hell out of folks*
> *Than all of the evangelists do.*

When he arrived in Nashville to join the WSM Barn Dance (it wasn't called the Grand Ole Opry until later) in 1925, Uncle Dave, like most of his fellow Tennesseans, was still talking about the summer's "monkey trial" at Dayton, Tennessee, where a young teacher named John T. Scopes had been found guilty of the crime of teaching evolution at Dayton's high school. The guilty verdict brought a $100 fine and orders to pay court costs. Many thought he had got off too easy.

In those days of story songs based on headlines, Macon's reaction was to write and sing a song he titled, "The Bible's True." It was a rollicking, hand-clapping evangelistic tune:

Evolution teaches man came from a monkey,
I don't believe no such thing in the days of a
  week of Sundays.

Chorus:
For the Bible's true, yes I believe it,
I've seen enough and I can prove it,
What you say, what you say, it's bound to be that way.

God made the world and everything that's in it,
He made man perfect and the monkey wasn't in it.
(repeat chorus)

I'm no evolutionist that wants the world to see,
There can't no man from anywhere, boys, make a
   monkey out of me.
(repeat chorus)

God made the world, and then He made man,
Woman for his helpmate, beat that if you can.
(repeat chorus)

Uncle Dave had his audience singing along with him on the choruses before he finished. But it must be said that he brought the same enthusiasm to his secular songs, some of them a bit naughty: "Keep My Skillet Good and Greasy," "Old Maid's Last Hope (A Burglar Song)," "(She Was Always) Chewing Gum," "I Tickled Nancy," "Kissin' On the Sly," and "She's Got Money, Too."

But whether at the Opry or on tour, Macon had gospel songs in his performance. He preferred the standards of the genre: "One More River to Cross," "Shall We Gather At the River?," "When the Roll Is Called Up Yonder," "In the Sweet Bye and Bye," "Nearer My God to Thee," "Sweet Hour of Prayer."

Comedienne Minnie Pearl recalled her times with Uncle Dave while on the road with the Grand Ole Opry tent show: "We would often sit in the back of the tent when others were performing, and Uncle Dave would talk of religion. He complained about ministers departing from the Bible. He could quote at great length from Scripture and used it to present solutions to all the problems of the world."

When David Harrison Macon died at the age of eighty-two in 1952, his Grand Ole Opry friends erected a monument to him on a hillside just outside of Woodbury, Tennessee, overlooking U. S. Route 70, the road on which Uncle Dave used to drive his mule-drawn freight wagons. A banjo was carved on the stone, with a likeness of Macon, and the title of one of his favorite hymns: "How Beautiful Heaven Must Be."

It is part of the considerable and colorful lore of country music that on the last day of July, 1927—a Sunday—a Model A Ford left the tiny Clinch Mountain community of Maces Spring, Virginia, to embark on a twenty-five-mile drive over rough dirt roads to the town of Bristol, sitting astride the Virginia-Tennessee border. At the wheel was a tall, stern-faced man named A. P. "Doc" Carter, and with him in the car was his wife, Sara, who held their suckling baby, Joe; an eight-year-old daughter, Gladys, and Doc's sister-in-law, Maybelle, who was seven months pregnant. Musical instruments filled the remaining space in the small car.

They were responding to a newspaper announcement placed by Ralph Peer, an itinerant recording pioneer who worked for the Victor Talking Machine Company. On August first and second, Doc, Sara, and Maybelle cut six songs on Peer's portable equipment, which had been set up in a makeshift studio on the Tennessee side of Bristol's State Street.

Few artists have had the influence on country music that can be attributed to the Carter Family. In a very real sense, that applies to gospel music as well. Doc Carter played the fiddle, but not really very well. The stern religious beliefs of his family prohibited him from playing what were considered worldly dance jigs. And those beliefs led to a marriage of traditional hill country folk songs and hill country gospel tunes. It was a marriage that continues to this very day.

They had a strong preference for religious songs. As Professor Bill Malone wrote in his landmark history, *Country Music, U. S. A.:* "Most of the Carters' religious songs, originating in the fundamentalist tradition, stressed the importance of holiness, emphasized the sadness and wickedness of this life, and related the joys of the heavenly home beyond the grave. . . .

"For example, the well-known 'Will the Circle Be Unbroken,' tells of a heart-broken person who follows the hearse as it carries his mother to the burial ground. Although the words may be maudlin, they are not unrealistic. They sprang from and were representative of a Victorian culture which was acutely conscious of death and the sorrow it could bring to tightly-knit family groups."

In the late sixties, the Carter Family (meaning then Maybelle and her three daughters—Helen, June, and Anita) became associated with the country megastar Johnny Cash, and Mother Maybelle, known widely for her unique guitar style, had another resurgence of national recognition on network television. Cash married June Carter in 1968.

John R. Cash was a child of the Depression in the South, which was vastly different from the Depression in northern industrial cities. From the age of three to eighteen, Johnny lived in Dyess, Arkansas, a community born of necessity during the Great Depression, brought into being by the federal government to resettle poor families who needed the promised twenty acres of delta land, the mule, and the small frame house provided just to survive. The roads of the settlement dedicated to raising cotton didn't have names; in true bureaucratic efficiency they were simply numbered. The Cashes lived on Road Three.

Attendance at the Road Fifteen Church of God, where Johnny was taken by his mother as a little boy, wasn't enjoyable at first. "The thing I remember most," he was to write in his autobiography, "was fear. I didn't understand it as worship then. . . . The preacher terrified me. He shouted and cried and gasped. The longer he preached, the louder he got and the more he gasped for breath. . . . But the people were caught up in the fever. . . . The writhing on the floor, the moaning, the trembling, and the jerks they got into scared me even more. . . .

"At the time I could see no joy in what they were doing. (But) I can still see my mother's look of joy and happiness each time we left the church. And by the time I was five or six years old, I didn't dread it as much. I went willingly."

What fascinated the youngster was that all kinds of musical instruments—guitar, mandolin, banjo—were used in the services. "As far as I was concerned, the service might as well have ended when the songs were over. Because it was the songs I was beginning to feel."

Johnny Cash was to take those impressions into his adult life. In Memphis, at the storied Sun Record Company where Elvis Presley, Jerry Lee Lewis, Carl Perkins, and Charlie Rich were being molded into stars, the door was opened to Cash's career as a performer. Three years later, when Columbia Records signed him, he was able to record his first gospel album, which featured his own song, written in 1958:

Lead me, Father, with the staff of life,
And give the strength for a song.
The word I sing
Might more strength bring,
To help some poor troubled weary worker along.

Frederick E. Danker, writing in *Stars of Country Music,* said Johnny's "early albums of hymns, while following the custom that country artists should cut such collections every year or two . . . reveal a more convincing (even passionate) identification with this kind of song than was the norm, except among strictly gospel singers.''

However, Cash's stardom was to come in the secular field, with such hits as ''Folsom Prison Blues,'' ''I Got Stripes,'' ''Give Me Love to Rose,'' ''Hey, Porter,'' ''Rock Island Line,'' ''Orange Blossom Special,'' ''Don't Take Your Guns to Town,'' ''I Walk the Line,'' ''Guess Things Happen That Way,'' ''Ways of a Woman In Love,'' ''Jackson,'' ''If I Were A Carpenter''—and on and on.

The road to his stardom, though, was filled with potholes of amphetamines and alcohol. His health suffered severely. There was one particularly disagreeable incident at the Grand Ole Opry, where, high on pills, he irrationally dragged a microphone stand along the stage footlights, popping fifty or sixty bulbs, the broken glass shattering all over the stage and into the audience. He was summarily fired from the Opry and it is no exaggeration to say that his career was an eyelash away from ruin.

But in 1968, his personal life was turned around. He defeated his drug problem with the constant help of Dr. Nat Winston, June Carter, and June's parents, Maybelle and Ezra Carter. Slowly and surely he turned to more and more gospel projects.

He produced a movie called *Gospel Road,* the story of Jesus told and sung; a movie carrying the identification mark of his music as well as being a vivid expression of his faith. He wrote a novel about the conversion of the Apostle Paul, before and after, titled *Man In White,* a switch on the title of his autobiography, *Man In Black.* He and June have made numerous singing and testifying appearances at the crusades of evangelist Billy Graham. And the House of Cash song catalog includes the likes of ''He Turned the Water Into

Wine," "Land of Israel," "Come to the Wailing Wall," "No Earthly Good," and "My Children Walk In Truth."

Now, in 1994, there has been another turn in Johnny Cash's road. He has a new recording contract with American Records, one that gives him creative control over what he records—something he has not really had in his long career. His first new album reflects his folk, blues, and *gospel* heritage. Those who know him best believe the gospel will be predominant.

Thus, country music's history is replete with its gospel connection.

Probably no country music singer has sold more gospel albums than did Tennessee Ernie Ford, the "Old Pea Picker," who was justly famous for his secular hit, "Sixteen Tons." But his sales records for religious albums topped ten million! In 1965, the National Academy of Recording Arts & Sciences gave Ford its prestigious Grammy Award for "Great Gospel Songs," an album he cut with Nashville's Jordanaires quartet.

Country music Hall of Famer Eddy Arnold released more than a few gospel albums during his long association with RCA Victor, including one titled "Praise Him, Praise Him," a superb tribute to legendary hymnwriter Fanny Crosby.

His fellow Hall of Famer, Bill Monroe, the acknowledged "Father of Blue Grass," had his early training with a shaped note teacher in his native Kentucky. And his repertoire has always included gospel songs, including his first hit recording in 1936 of "What You Give In Exchange (For Your Soul)?" But his hillbilly tenor is also regularly heard on "Lord, Build Me A Cabin In Glory," "A Voice From On High," "I'll Meet You In Church Sunday Morning," "River of Death," "I'm

Working On a Building,'' and ''Walking In Jerusa-lem.'' There are those who contend that it is the purest form of country gospel around today.

Kris Kristofferson, who won the Country Music Association's Best Song of the Year award in 1970 for ''Sunday Morning Coming Down,'' which definitely was *not* a gospel song, crossed genres when he also won the Gospel Music Association's Dove Award in 1973 as the composer of ''Why Me Lord?'' Two years later he won the gospel song of the year award again with ''One Day At A Time,'' co-written with Marijohn Wilkin, another writer with considerable country music credits.

Another crossover writer and performer has been Jimmie Davis, who parlayed the immense success of his ''You Are My Sunshine'' into two terms as governor of Louisiana. And into the Country Music Hall of Fame. As early as 1934, he wrote ''When It's Round-Up Time In Heaven.'' He also co-wrote ''How Far Is Heaven?'' (with Tillman Franks) and ''A Sinner's Prayer'' (with Alberta NcEnery). After his political career was ended, Davis toured widely as a gospel singer. In 1957, more than a decade before the GMA's Dove Awards, a music trade journal named him ''the best male sacred singer of the year.''

It is not widely recalled today, but Texan Willie Nelson, composer of such country classics as ''Crazy,'' ''Hello Walls,'' ''Funny How Time Slips Away,'' ''Night Life,'' and ''On the Road Again,'' had as his first hit a song titled ''Family Bible,'' recorded by one Claude Gray.

Then, too, there have been two notable close-harmony male quartets who for many years have been predominantly positioned astride the boundary line between gospel and country: The Oak Ridge Boys and The Statler Brothers.

The Oak Ridge Boys have gospel roots, going back to 1945, in the mountains of East Tennessee. They were basically gospel at first, but played a large role in the development of a "mod" sound in the gospel field. With the venerable Brock Speer as their producer, the Oaks were part of what is believed to be the first major gospel recording session in Nashville, using brass, strings, and "Nashville Sound" arrangements. The result was a trend-setting album, *Music City, USA,* released by Skylite Records.

When the Dove Awards began in 1969 the Oak Ridge Boys's *It's Happening* (a prophetic title for the group) was named album of the year. Now they were on the HeartWarming label and were produced by the veteran Bob MacKenzie. In 1972, they won the same award again for their album, *Light,* repeating in 1973 with *Street Gospel,* perhaps the first deliberate urbanization of the gospel music message. The Oaks were the hottest act around in gospel music then, also being named the male group of the year in 1970 and 1972 (there were no Dove Awards in 1971).

But in those days, "hot" in gospel music did not necessarily equate with "hot" in the bank account. The act faced bankruptcy. Duane Allen, who had been an Oak Ridge Boy since 1968, led them out of the fiscal woods. Cautiously at first, they began a switch to country music, adapting their upbeat gospel quartet harmony to the different genre. In 1977, their recording of "Y'All Come Back Saloon" broke the country hit ice. Other hits followed: "Sail Away," "Dream On," "You're the One In A Million," "Elvira," "Bobby Sue," "So Fine," "Thank God for Kids," "America Made," "I Guess It Never Hurts to Hurt Sometimes,"

"Touch A Hand, Make A Friend," "An American Family," "Change My Mind," "Baby On Board."

And they've never been far from their gospel roots. Concerts include gospel songs. Bass singer Richard Sterban sang with The Stamps Quartet, which backed Elvis Presley for a time, and joined the Oaks in 1972. Tenor Joe Bonsall was a Philadelphia street gang kid before singing with the Keystones gospel group; another member of the Keystones was Sterban. Joe joined the Oaks in 1973. And the newest Oak Ridge Boy (joining the quartet in 1987), Steve Sanders, was a child star in gospel music under the handle of "Little Stevie Sanders."

The Statler Brothers, who took their stage name from a box of facial tissues, are of the gospel heritage of Virginia. They started in Staunton, Virginia, and still headquarter there. There *are* brothers in the act but their name isn't Statler; it's Don and Harold Reid. And the quartet has been remarkably stable in personnel over the years, unlike many male quartets. There's been only one change in the group since they won two Grammy Awards in 1965: for best new country and western group and best contemporary performance by a group. At that time the act included the two Reids, Phil Balsley, and Lew DeWitt. When poor health brought a retirement by DeWitt in the early 1980s, tenor Jimmy Fortune came aboard and is still there.

What especially distinguishes the Statlers' act is that they all are songwriters. Very little of what they record—and they have numerous gold and platinum albums—is by outside writers.

Harold Reid, the quartet's bass singer, explained their songwriting: "I think it's mid-America country music. We don't do drinkin' songs; we don't do cheatin' songs. We do what we consider everyday *emotion* songs. These songs touch on those everyday emotions or those everyday memories that Mr. and Mrs. America have run up on or have.''

They must be on the right track because they have won no less than forty-nine *Music City News* awards, in which the public does the polling. While touring for a time with Johnny Cash in the mid-sixties helped their appeal, it can be said that the Statler Brothers made their own way.

Their hit songs have been unending: ''Flowers On the Wall,'' ''Class of '57,'' ''Do You Remember These?,'' ''Monday Morning Secretary,'' ''Woman Without A Home,'' ''Oh, Baby Mine,'' ''Do You Know You Are My Sunshine?,'' ''Thank You World,'' ''I'll Go to My Grave Loving You,'' ''Pictures,'' ''Susan When She Tried,'' ''Whatever Happened to Randolph Scott?,'' ''Elizabeth,'' ''One Takes the Blame,'' ''Count On Me,'' ''More Than Just A Name on the Wall''—the list goes on. And on.

Always, though, the Statlers maintain their firm gospel connection in concerts. ''If we don't do 'How Great Thou Art,' '' Don Reid says, ''I'd think we'd be stoned out of the building. We do it and we love to do it, not only because we love the song but because the people want to hear [it].''

The people have also bought more than a million copies of a special gospel album collection by the Statlers. And the people have made the Statler Brothers television variety hour each Saturday night on The Nashville Network (TNN) the highest rated show on the cable channel. The Statlers end every week by gathering around a piano and closing the show with a gospel song.

In the spring of 1994 came another example of a major crossover to gospel—by Charlie Daniels, the unchallenged leader of southern country rock. After twenty-four albums in his distinctive hard-driving, energy-laden style, dating back to 1970, Daniels has released his first gospel album without changing his style at all.

Titled *The Door*, the album has been released by one of the biggest companies in the gospel field, Sparrow Records. Included in the album is a new song by southern gospel legend Joel Hemphill ("Two Out of Three") and a song Daniels co-wrote with multiple Grammy and Dove awards winner Steven Curtis Chapman ("The Business of Love").

Daniels, who has personally promoted the album on every available television and radio talk show, has been totally candid about the album: "I'm not preaching to the choir. What I want to do is basically talk to the old boy who comes in at 5:00 Sunday morning hung over and turns the TV on to a church program. Everything just looks too 'holy' to him. He says, 'I can't ever be part of that. I don't understand that.'

"I want to talk to him because Jesus died for him too. In fact, the song on the album, 'Jesus Died For You,' says, 'You may think you can't cope/You may be drunk or hooked on dope/Believe me brother, you've got hope/'Cause Jesus died for you.' If people could hear only one song, I would want it to be 'Jesus Died For You.' That's the crux of this album. That's what it's all about. I want to talk to people that nobody talks to."

There is no question that *The Door* album is powerful. Charlie addresses present-day mores in a song titled "Praying to the Wrong God":

You've got your mansion out on millionaire's row
Go all the places that the rich folks go
Your Bible is a checkbook and your church is a bank

But you're praying to the wrong God mister
You're living for your sensual pleasures and your
  evil desires
Praying to the wrong God mister
One of these days it's going to eat your flesh like fire.

This album will not be embraced by everyone. But, in time, it may be regarded as the most important country-to-gospel musical "conversion" in several decades.

Afterword

GOSPEL SINGER AMY GRANT, HERSELF A FOUR-TIME Gospel Music Association Artist of the Year, stood before a packed audience gathered in Nashville's Grand Ole Opry House, and simultaneously before a national television audience, told her listeners, "Gospel is more than a musical style, it's a life-giving message."

What followed on that Thursday evening of April 28, 1994, was a glittering TV show on the Family Channel observing the twenty-fifth anniversary of the GMA's Dove Awards, given to honor the best in gospel music. Most of the faces seen on the telecast were young and bright, not unlike Ms. Grant's own, attesting to the new vigor that has come to gospel music in the past decade.

The telecast itself was carefully crafted to be a two-hour promotion for the gospel music industry (for that is what it has become). So, too, were the well-produced commercials, largely an array of messages from national Christian bookstore chains, believed to be a joint $500-million-a-year enterprise, and more. In sum, the Dove Awards demonstrated that gospel music—as a business—is alive and well and prosperous in America today.

Yet, perhaps there was a missed opportunity, given the fact that this was the twenty-fifth anniversary show, suggesting a need to remember gospel music's colorful heritage—to remember the people what brung 'em, to resort to the vernacular.

171

True, there were two short spots in the show somewhat making that effort. One was the appearance of Shirley Caesar, who, with choir backing, delivered a rousing version of "God Again," which paid homage to the black gospel element of the multifaceted music.

And then there was the spot with the excellent Bill Gaither Vocal Band, introduced to give a platform for such venerable folks as bass singer Armond Morales, Vestal Goodman, the very first female gospel vocalist of the year back in 1969, and the great Jake Hess, an early southern gospel quartet singer and creator of a sound with the Imperials quartet that bridged the gap between the traditional and the contemporary. Together they performed a moving rendition of "Glory," which stirred the audience to its feet with an ovation for the first time in the telecast.

But one can wonder whether that was enough for a twenty-fifth anniversary show. Might not a place have been found, for example, for the Singing Speer Family, Dove Award winners in the first eight years? The Speers, of course, are still active.

As a television producer myself for nearly forty years, I understand that television time is finite. I also understand the "rule" which says that the audience most sought by the advertisers on TV is in the 18-to-35 age range. But sometimes, even with those strictures, rules can be broken (and should have been on this occasion), making way for the drama that would have been inherent in the twenty-fifth anniversary appearance of the Speers.

That criticism aside, the evening of April 28, 1994, clearly belonged to young Michael English, a highly popular solo entertainer and a member of the Gaither Vocal Band. His talents gave him a role in no less than six Dove Awards. He was named both the male vocalist of the year and the gospel music artist of the year; his

album, titled *Hope*—only his second—won the Dove
as the best contemporary album of 1993.

Further, "Holding Out Hope to You," a song from
English's album written by Joe Beck, Brian White, and
David Wills, won a Dove for the inspirational recorded
song of the year. Then, too, his work with the Gaither
Vocal Band brought English two more Dove Awards:
for best southern gospel album, *Southern Classics,* and
for best southern gospel recorded song, "Satisfied."

For that evening at least, the world was Michael English's oyster and he was the pearl found therein. He
was genuinely moved by the honors coming his way,
telling the audience: "I would not be on this stage
tonight if it wasn't for Bill and Gloria Gaither tutoring
me, teaching me." And he added: "God has blessed
me. And I hope to do what God wants me to do, whatever it is."

Later, backstage, English acknowledged to reporters
that his career has been marked with anxiety attacks
about his performances but explained how he gains
strength from his continuing insecurity. "I like being
where I don't believe that much in myself," he said.
"That's how I know that God is my strength, and that's
the only way I'm going to survive."

Just one week later, with the irony of his award-
night comments echoing in every ear along Nashville's
storied Music Row, his record label, Warner Alliance,
released a tersely worded, and somewhat ambiguous,
statement from English.

It read: "I feel it is necessary to announce my with-
drawal from the Christian music industry because of
mistakes that I have recently made. Although I am very
much appreciative of the support I have received from
those involved in Christian music, I feel it necessary to
relinquish the Dove Awards that I was honored with
this past week.

"I am a human being and I have failed. I ask your forgiveness.

"These circumstances are obviously the hardest I have had to face in my life, and I would hope that you will support me and all the persons involved with your prayers."

The ambiguity of the statement didn't last long; within twenty-four hours it was revealed, and confirmed by several sources, that English, a married man, had been involved in an affair with another gospel singer, Marabeth Jordan, also married, and that she was pregnant with English's child.

More than one source along Music Row made the point that such a circumstance in the secular music world would have hardly raised an eyebrow these days. But it is different in the realm of gospel music. Warner Alliance, for example, immediately announced that it would stop all promotion, marketing, and sales of Michael English's pop-influenced inspirational music.

On the Sunday following the English revelations, a scene played out at the large Christ Church, Nashville's largest and best known Pentecostal church—the spiritual home of many of the music world's stars. On that day the big choir led the congregation in the singing of the "old hymns," notably "Amazing Grace," "The Old Rugged Cross," and "How Great Thou Art." It seemed to be a reaffirmation of the traditional values of Christian music while, at the same time, making a statement of doubt about the proliferation of "pop" gospel.

Perhaps choir director Landy Gardner said it best. "This has been an eventful week, to say the least," he told reporters, tears welling in his eyes. "We as human beings love to find heroes; we elevate people to places they don't belong. We need to learn the lesson and put our trust in the One who is faithful."

There is no question that contemporary Christian music has become big business in recent years; some sources say it has developed into a $1 billion dollar giant, given muscle by record company promoters, press agents, and management companies that previously toiled only in the vineyards of secular music.

In one sense Michael English's personal tragedy may yet serve to marry the energy of the contemporary gospel movement to the traditions of the music. For down through the years, from Fanny Crosby and Ira Sankey and Homer Rodeheaver and The Stamps and The Speers and The Blackwoods and The LeFevres and Georgia Tom Dorsey and Mahalia Jackson and George Beverly Shea—and so many others—the gospel music torch has been kept lit. And it still burns brightly today.

Christian music remains resilient in the thousands of performers who continue to heed the Biblical admonition:

> *Sing to Him a new song;*
> *Play skillfully with a shout of joy.*

Bibliography

Blackwell, Lois S. *The Wings of the Dove: The Story of Gospel Music in America.* Norfolk, Virginia: The Donning Company, 1978.

Burt, Jesse, and Duane Allen. *The History of Gospel Music.* Nashville: K & S Press, 1971.

Cash, Johnny. *Man In Black.* Grand Rapids, Michigan: Zondervan Publishing House, 1975.

Crosby, Fanny J. *Memories of Eighty Years.* Boston: James H. Earle Co., 1906.

————. *Fanny Crosby's Story of Ninety-Four Years.* New York: Fleming H. Revell Company, 1914.

Cusic, Don. "Sandi Patti." *BMI Magazine,* No. 1 (1984), pp. 46-47.

Danker, Frederic E. *Stars of Country Music.* Chicago: University of Illinois Press, 1975.

Gaither, Bill, w Jerry Jenkins. *I Almost Missed the Sunset: My Perspectives On Life and Music.* Nashville: Thomas Nelson Publishers, 1992.

Granger, Thom. "Steven Curtis Chapman's Excellent Adventure." *Contemporary Christian Music,* July (1992), pp. 50-53.

Hagan, Chet. *Country Music Legends in the Hall of Fame.* Nashville: Thomas Nelson Publishers, 1982.

————. *Grand Ole Opry.* New York: Henry Holt & Company, 1989.

Hall, J. H. *Biographies of Gospel Song and Hymn Writers.* New York: Fleming H. Revell Company, 1914.

Harris, Michael W. *The Rise of Gospel Blues: The*

Music of Thomas Andrew Dorsey in the Urban Church. New York: Oxford University Press, 1992.

Heilbut, Anthony. *The Gospel Sound: Good News and Bad Times.* New York: Limelight Editions, 1985.

Hughes, Langston. *Famous Negro Music Makers.* New York: Dodd, Mead & Company, 1955.

————, and Arna Bontemps. *The Book of Negro Folklore.* New York: Dodd, Mead & Company, 1958.

The Ira D. Sankey Centenary: Proceedings of the Centenary Celebration. New Castle, Pennsylvania: Lawrence County Historical Society, 1941.

Malone, Bill C. *Country Music, U.S.A.: A Fifty-Year History.* Austin, Texas: For the American Folklore Society by the University of Texas Press, 1969.

————, and Judith McCulloh. *Stars of Country Music.* Urbana, Illinois: University of Illinois Press, 1955.

McLoughlin, William G., Jr. *Billy Sunday Was His Real Name.* Chicago: University of Chicago Press, 1955.

Miller, Basil. *Ten Singers Who Became Famous.* Grand Rapids, Michigan: Zondervan Publishing House, 1954.

Minnix, Kathleen. *Laughter in the Amen Corner: The Life of Evangelist Sam Jones.* Athens, Georgia: University of Georgia Press, 1993.

O'Neal, Jim, and Amy O'Neal. "Georgia Tom Dorsey." *Living Blues,* Vol. 20 (1975), pp. 17-34.

Porter, T. N. "Homer Alvan Rodeheaver: Evangelistic Musician and Publisher." Doctoral Dissertation, New Orleans Baptist Theological Seminary, 1981.

Price, Deborah Evans. "Gospel Songwriter of the Year." *American Songwriter,* July/August (1989), pp. 11-24-29.

————. "Twila Paris: Creating Musical Garments." American Songwriter, March/April (1994), pp. 10-11, 16-17.

Reagon, Bernice Johnson. *We'll Understand It Better*

By and By: Pioneering African American Gospel Composers. Washington: Smithsonian Institution Press, 1992.

Rodeheaver, Homer. *Twenty Years with Billy Sunday*. Winona Lake, Indiana: The Rodeheaver Hall-Mack Company, 1936.

———. *Singing Black: Twenty Thousand Miles with a Music Missionary*. Chicago: Rodeheaver Co., 1936.

Schwerin, Jules. *Got To Tell It: Mahalia Jackson, Queen of Gospel*. New York: Oxford University Press, 1992.

Shea, George Beverly, with Fred Bauer. *Then Sings My Soul*. Old Tappan, New Jersey: Fleming H. Ravell Company, 1968.

———, with Fred Bauer. *Songs That Lift the Heart*. Old Tappan, New Jersey: Fleming H. Ravell Company, 1972.

Shellenberger, Susie. "Christmas With Twila," *Brio*, December (1993), pp. 18-22.

Amazing and Inspiring True Stories of Divine Intervention

They are with us always...

ANGELS   72331-X/$4.99 US
  by Hope Price

ANGELS AMONG US   77377-5/$4.99 US/$5.99 Can
  by Don Fearheiley

They happen when you least expect them
and need them most...

MIRACLES   77652-9/$4.99 US/$5.99 Can
  by Don Fearheiley

The Best in Biographies from Avon Books

IT'S ALWAYS SOMETHING
by Gilda Radner   71072-2/ $5.95 US/ $6.95 Can

RUSH!
by Michael Arkush
                      77539-5/ $4.99 US/ $5.99 Can

STILL TALKING
by Joan Rivers   71992-4/ $5.99 US/ $6.99 Can

CARY GRANT: THE LONELY HEART
by Charles Higham and Roy Moseley
                      71099-9/ $5.99 US/ $6.99 Can

I, TINA
by Tina Turner and Kurt Loder
                      70097-2/ $5.99 US/ $7.99 Can

ONE MORE TIME
by Carol Burnett   70449-8/ $4.95 US/ $5.95 Can

PATTY HEARST: HER OWN STORY
by Patricia Campbell Hearst with Alvin Moscow
                      70651-2/ $5.99 US/ $6.99 Can

SPIKE LEE
by Alex Patterson   76994-8/ $4.99 US/ $5.99 Can